SUPPLIER RELATIONSHIP MANAGEMENT

HOW TO MAXIMIZE VENDOR VALUE AND OPPORTUNITY

Christian Schuh

Michael F. Strohmer

Stephen Easton

Mike Hales

Alenka Triplat

Supplier Relationship Management: How to Maximize Vendor Value and Opportunity

ISBN-13 (pbk): 978-1-4302-6259-6

ISBN-13 (electronic): 978-1-4302-6260-2

Trademarked names, logos, and images may appear in this book. Rather than use a trademark symbol with every occurrence of a trademarked name, logo, or image we use the names, logos, and images only in an editorial fashion and to the benefit of the trademark owner, with no intention of infringement of the trademark.

The use in this publication of trade names, trademarks, service marks, and similar terms, even if they are not identified as such, is not to be taken as an expression of opinion as to whether or not they are subject to proprietary rights.

While the advice and information in this book are believed to be true and accurate at the date of publication, neither the authors nor the editors nor the publisher can accept any legal responsibility for any errors or omissions that may be made. The publisher makes no warranty, expressed or implied, with respect to the material contained herein.

Publisher: Heinz Weinheimer
Acquisitions Editor: Jeff Olson
Editorial Board: Steve Anglin, Mark Beckner, Ewan Buckingham, Gary Cornell,
    Louise Corrigan, James DeWolf, Jonathan Gennick, Jonathan Hassell,
    Robert Hutchinson, Michelle Lowman, James Markham, Matthew Moodie, Jeff Olson,
    Jeffrey Pepper, Douglas Pundick, Ben Renow-Clarke, Dominic Shakeshaft,
    Gwenan Spearing, Matt Wade, Steve Weiss
Coordinating Editor: Rita Fernando
Copy Editor: Jana Weinstein
Compositor: SPi Global
Indexer: SPi Global
Cover Designer: Tomaž Nečemar

Distributed to the book trade worldwide by Springer Science+Business Media New York, 233 Spring Street, 6th Floor, New York, NY 10013. Phone 1-800-SPRINGER, fax (201) 348-4505, e-mail orders-ny@springer-sbm.com, or visit www.springeronline.com. Apress Media, LLC is a California LLC and the sole member (owner) is Springer Science + Business Media Finance Inc (SSBM Finance Inc). SSBM Finance Inc is a **Delaware** corporation.

For information on translations, please e-mail rights@apress.com, or visit www.apress.com.

Apress and friends of ED books may be purchased in bulk for academic, corporate, or promotional use. eBook versions and licenses are also available for most titles. For more information, reference our Special Bulk Sales–eBook Licensing web page at www.apress.com/bulk-sales.

Any source code or other supplementary materials referenced by the author in this text is available to readers at www.apress.com. For detailed information about how to locate your book's source code, go to www.apress.com/source-code/.

Apress Business: The Unbiased Source of Business Information

Apress business books provide essential information and practical advice, each written for practitioners by recognized experts. Busy managers and professionals in all areas of the business world—and at all levels of technical sophistication—look to our books for the actionable ideas and tools they need to solve problems, update and enhance their professional skills, make their work lives easier, and capitalize on opportunity.

Whatever the topic on the business spectrum—entrepreneurship, finance, sales, marketing, management, regulation, information technology, among others—Apress has been praised for providing the objective information and unbiased advice you need to excel in your daily work life. Our authors have no axes to grind; they understand they have one job only—to deliver up-to-date, accurate information simply, concisely, and with deep insight that addresses the real needs of our readers.

It is increasingly hard to find information—whether in the news media, on the Internet, and now all too often in books—that is even-handed and has your best interests at heart. We therefore hope that you enjoy this book, which has been carefully crafted to meet our standards of quality and unbiased coverage.

We are always interested in your feedback or ideas for new titles. Perhaps you'd even like to write a book yourself. Whatever the case, reach out to us at editorial@apress.com and an editor will respond swiftly. Incidentally, at the back of this book, you will find a list of useful related titles. Please visit us at www.apress.com to sign up for newsletters and discounts on future purchases.

The Apress Business Team

This book is dedicated to our clients

Contents

About the Authors

Christian Schuh has led procurement transformation projects for clients in the automotive, construction equipment, defense, high-tech, packaging, and steel industries in Europe, Russia, China, and the US. He is the author of various books on procurement (most notably *The Purchasing Chessboard* and *The CPO*), monographs, and articles. Christian studied aeronautical engineering at the Graz University of Technology and holds a doctorate in business administration. He lives in the historic city center of Vienna.

Michael F. Strohmer is an expert on raw material strategies, procurement transformation, post-merger management, and large-scale CAPEX projects. His work encompasses the utilities, automotive and defense sectors, consumer goods, packaging, and steel. He has published several books (including *The Purchasing Chessboard* and *The CPO*) and articles, and he is a frequent speaker at international conferences. Michael holds doctorate degrees in business administration and law. He lives in Austria's picturesque lake region near Salzburg.

Stephen Easton is a specialist on improving the effectiveness of external procurement activities. He has supported a number of both private and public sector clients in achieving significant and sustained financial results. Stephen is coauthor of *The CPO*. He has an MBA from Cornell University and a first degree in politics, philosophy, and economics from the University of Oxford. He lives in Surrey, southwest of London.

Mike Hales has over 35 years of industry and consulting experience working in North America, South America, Europe, and Asia Pacific. His global cross-industry experience covers all aspects of operations; support services; sales channels; customer experience; and merger integration. He has a special focus on expanding the impact of procurement from sourcing to supplier relationship management. He has contributed to over 20 articles on procurement, innovation, customer experience, and channel strategy. He serves on the Board of Directors for The Chicago Council on Global Affairs, and the Board of Trustees for the Institute of Supply Management's Center for Strategic Supply Leadership. He is coauthor of the *Global Cities Index*, which ranks cities worldwide based on their global engagement. He holds a bachelor of science degree in business with honors from the University of North Carolina at Chapel Hill and a master's degree in management with honors from the Kellogg Graduate School of Management at Northwestern University. He lives in Chicago.

Alenka Triplat is a member of A.T. Kearney's Operations Practice. In the ten years she has spent with the firm in Vienna, she has led multiple projects on supply management topics across various industries, such as discrete manufacturing (consumer electronics, food consumer products, and heavy equipment); process industries (steel, gas, cables, and packaging); and financial institutions (commercial banks and insurances). She has worked with international clients based in most European countries and spent longer periods of time working and living in the US, China, and Taiwan. She is an expert on a wide range of supply management topics including sourcing strategies using the Purchasing Chessboard, negotiation techniques, and procurement transformation as well as cross-functional collaboration and manufacturing excellence. She has published multiple articles on these topics. Alenka studied economics at the University of Ljubljana (Slovenia) and business administration at Vienna University of Economics and Business Administration (Austria). She currently shuttles between Taipei, Vienna, and Ljubljana.

Preface

It is quite unusual to find white space on the map of a field as thoroughly researched as procurement. Therefore, it took us some time to understand how enormous the white space of supplier relationship management, or SRM, actually is. Indeed, the reader may well even question this assertion, given that SRM is hardly a new term. It has been talked and written about for decades and it has been applied in many ways. Sometimes it is even taken as synonymous for procurement itself. The closer we looked at SRM though, the bigger our fascination with the subject became. Just consider the careless use of the word *partner*. What exactly qualifies a supplier as a partner? Is a supplier that consumes a large share of a company's budget and provides excellent service at highly competitive prices a partner? And even if one business unit, one functional entity, or one hierarchy level thinks so, does the remainder of the company agree and does it manage the relationship to this alleged partner in a consistent way? And again, what is SRM anyway?

In truth, SRM really is a white space in the sense that everyone talks about it, and many companies have implemented features of it, but hardly any organization has put in place a comprehensive approach to driving value from it. The final push came from a CPO roundtable in New York City in April 2013. We quizzed the 50 CPOs present, who represent many of the most prestigious American businesses, with some of the previous questions. Their response was eye-opening—most of them identified SRM as a top-priority item, and none of them had seen any convincing approach to solve it. Before we knew it, we were totally absorbed by the subject and found ourselves dedicating spare minutes to SRM whenever we could. The result of our work in understanding and implementing SRM is this book.

In this endeavor we were fortunately not alone. We also owe a great debt to many of our past and current colleagues at A.T. Kearney, who have been at the forefront of developing effective procurement practice over the years. Due to space considerations, we have to limit acknowledgements to those who gave us the most valuable assistance, both as discussion partners and as rich sources of ideas: Íñigo Aranzabal (Madrid), Johan Aurik (Brussels), John Blascovich (New York), Reuben Chaudhury (New York), Laurent Chevreux (Paris), Johnson Chng (Hong Kong), Mark Clouse (New York), Charles Davis (London), Fred Eng (New York),

Carrie Ericson (San Francisco), Kai Engel (Düsseldorf), Richard Forrest (London), Axel Freyberg (Berlin), Jennifer Garlitz (Washington, DC), Jules Goffre (Munich), Florian Haslauer (Vienna), Martin Haubensak (Düsseldorf), Rene Heller (Amsterdam), Terry Innerst (Sydney), Götz Klink (Stuttgart), Rick Kozole (Detroit), Robert Kromoser (Vienna), John Kurtz (Jakarta), Tobias Lewe (Düsseldorf), Alex Liu (San Francisco), Daniel Mahler (New York), Jessica Mahre (Atlanta), Federico Mariscotti (Dubai), Michael McCool (Hong Kong), Xavier Mesnard (Paris), Dietrich Neumann (Berlin), Joon Ooi (Singapore), Kurt Oswald (Vienna), Mark Page (London), Jim Pearce (London), Peter Pfeiffer (Düsseldorf), Wim Plaizier (Amsterdam), Thomas Rings (Munich), Joe Raudabaugh (Chicago), Enrico Rizzon (Melbourne), Luca Rossi (Milan), Marco Santino (Rome), Martin Sonnenschein (Berlin), Dan Starta (Dubai), Peter Scharbert (Munich), Oliver Scheel (Düsseldorf), Sieghart Scheiter (Düsseldorf), Otto Schulz (Düsseldorf), Wolfgang Steck (Zurich), Markus Stricker (Zurich), Fuminori Takemura (Tokyo), Yves Thill (Atlanta), Bart van Dijk (Johannesburg), Patrick van den Bossche (Washington), Jan van der Oord (Amsterdam), Mark van Weegen (Atlanta), Mirko Warschun (Munich), and Robyn Wright (London). Armin Scharlach from our Berlin office deserves a very special mention here for contributing the key input to the chapter on the role of IT in SRM. Our gratitude also goes out to our A. T. Kearney editorial team, especially Patricia Sibo, without whom this book would not have been possible. We also owe special gratitude to Jeff Olson, our editor at Apress, who has been as sympathetic and supportive of our ideas as ever. Last, but not least, Tomaž Nečemar designed the cover and we are highly appreciative of his design capabilities.

We are confident that this book will change the way companies deal with their suppliers in a way that ultimately benefits both parties. We hope it will encourage our readers to drive alignment across business units, functional entities, and hierarchy levels. Our hope is that you enjoy reading it as much as we enjoyed writing it.

Christian Schuh

Michael F. Strohmer

Stephen Easton

Mike Hales

Alenka Triplat

Procurement Success vs. SRM Failure

The Rise of Procurement

Let us be clear about one thing right from the start. This is not another book bashing procurement and calling out its allegedly many and obvious shortcomings. Over the past 20 years, procurement has made lots of great strides. A. T. Kearney's periodic study *Assessment of Excellence in Procurement* (AEP) speaks a clear language. Across industries and at a global level, procurement functions are in a pretty good shape.

Today, most companies do have a chief procurement officer (CPO) who has earned a seat at the table with his or her peers from innovation, production, marketing, sales, and finance. Given the high degree of focus on core competencies that can be observed consistently across industries, outsourcing of significant elements of the value chain has become the norm rather than the exception. This trend, more than anything, has fuelled what could be labeled as "the rise of the CPO." Strategic decisions about which product market segments to address and where and how to make products are driven rather than just supported by today's CPOs. And this modern CPO is more likely to overstress the term *customer value* than the term *cost savings*.

At the same time, functional silos have crumbled to ruins. Walk the corridors of any leading company and you are likely to see cross-functional teams working on key initiatives. Today's procurement executives are as eloquent in engineering and marketing language as their counterparts in the other functions are fluent in the language of sourcing strategies. The age-old tactic of suppliers playing functional managers against procurement people has largely lost its value and might even backfire on the suppliers.

Also, pounding the table has ceased to be the preferred sourcing strategy. Today's procurement teams are working with a host of differentiated strategies that are selected based on the company's demand power and the supplier's supply power. The resulting strategies exceed the traditional remit of procurement by far and pull in substantial competencies from engineering, manufacturing, IT, and supply chain management. They even encourage procurement people to think and act as entrepreneurs. A significant subset of the authors of this book hopes to have contributed to this trend with the creation of the Purchasing Chessboard.[1] This chessboard provides 64 techniques for buyers to reduce cost and increase value from category sourcing. These techniques are chosen depending on the balance between supply and demand power.

Managing operational processes has become a highly standardized topic. Today, no leading company worries about procure-to-pay processes. There is no more guessing and reinventing the wheel in these areas; there is just one right way to do it. The same is true for procurement information systems. After albeit huge investments, it has become the norm to press a key and get accurate information on who buys what from which supplier.

Procurement performance management is something of an exception, as it has seen more action recently. The advent of the financial ratio ROSMA (return on supply management assets) provides a way for procurement performance to be discussed in CFO-friendly terms. ROSMA provides the basis for gauging the financial performance of procurement with one single key performance indicator (KPI) and for managing the performance of procurement teams.

---

[1]Schuh, Christian, Robert Kromoser, Michael F. Strohmer, Joseph L. Raudabaugh, and Alenka Triplat. *The Purchasing Chessboard: 64 Methods to Reduce Costs and Increase Value with Suppliers*, 2nd ed. (Berlin: Springer, 2012).

With procurement organizations increasingly hiring talent over experience, procurement has become the intellectual hotbed for many companies. Droves of former management consultants and investment bankers team up with engineering, manufacturing, and marketing experts to overwhelm suppliers with data, facts, and analyses. Procurement people spend an increasing amount of time in internal academies and the senior executives leverage the advice of external coaches to help them perform better.

Everything Is Rosy, Then?

If everything was rosy, this would be a very short book and we could pack up and go home now. The one open issue we would like to point out is the inability of procurement executives to manage suppliers rather than categories. Most of the good things previously highlighted are totally category focused:

- The decisions on which product market segments to serve and where to produce goods are driven at a product or category level.

- Cross-functional teams working on the next hot products focus on categories and not on suppliers.

- All sourcing strategy development by definition is category-centric and not supplier-centric.

- Procurement performance management focuses on savings by category and product but hardly ever on the savings or value contributed by suppliers.

- And last, the talent recruited into procurement focuses on better understanding products and categories but hardly ever on managing suppliers.

Again, we are not advocating for stepping back on any of these points. Instead, we'd like to focus on the one important element that's missing. What we hear consistently from suppliers working with large customers are complaints about how hard it is to work with them. Suppliers are likely to get conflicting messages when working across business units (BUs). For example, one of us recalls the case of a machining supplier for a major aerospace business that constantly received mixed messages on how acceptable its quality and price performance were. Because the messages were not consistent, the supplier did not act. Then, one day the customer made the corporate decision to move business away lock, stock, and barrel. It gave the supplier no real opportunity to respond. This led directly to job losses and near closure of the affected plant.

All of us have also seen the curious case of one BU phasing out a supplier because it is unhappy with the overall performance of that supplier while another BU is increasing business with the very same supplier. Individually, there may be good reasons for that dichotomy, but in the grand scheme of things, this sends a very confusing message to the supplier.

The same lack of alignment can be observed across functions. Engineering may believe that a certain supplier is the greatest of all because it comes up with breakthrough technologies that will make a difference in the market. At the same time, manufacturing and supply chain managers may loath this specific supplier because it consistently fails in ramping up production and causes horrific quality problems. Again, all of us have seen suppliers that, despite disappointing day-to-day performance, get awarded with substantial new business.

Even worse is the frequent misalignment across hierarchy levels. Too many CEOs lack the time and discipline to ask for a thorough briefing before meeting a supplier. This sometimes leads to high-level conversations that only take place at the level of pure "relationship building" between individuals, without substantive content. Such a result at least does not cause harm. Far worse, lack of briefing can lead to agreements being made, or perceived to having been made, with a supplier that are completely counter to the real needs of the customer. We have all heard of examples where suppliers try to get CEOs to agree to things that look fine at a high level but that at a more detailed level would be soundly rejected. At the very least, what could be a fantastic opportunity to emphasize a message to a supplier becomes another cause of confusion that neither benefits the company nor the supplier.

Key Account Management vs. SRM

Let us repeat the observation that suppliers regard the internal misalignment of their customers as a problem rather than an opportunity. The conflicting messages they receive result in wasted effort for the supplier. Granted, some suppliers do cynically try to play "divide and rule." But, this is usually acquired or socialized behavior in response to the misalignment of the customer. A supplier is usually far happier if it can understand what the customer really expects with the minimum of effort.

Even the sophisticated key account-management routines that many suppliers have deployed fail to be a reliable remedy. After all, what good does it do to be very close to the key decision makers of your customer if they can't agree among themselves? A professional supplier will point out these inconsistencies to his customer to the degree that politeness permits. But there are limits to the extent of feedback a customer can digest, and too often, the supplier will have to cope with the fallout.

Therefore, we hear the suppliers' cry for supplier relationship management, or SRM. Professional suppliers prefer to work with customers who are aligned internally.

The Prize

What is SRM? While category management is all about the price of a product or service, SRM is about working more effectively with suppliers to deliver benefits. It recognizes that both parties need to achieve their goals. Today, SRM is instead often little more than the sum of all category management activities and infrequent executive-level meetings and hoping for the best.

Imagine the benefit companies could reap from opening up an additional dimension of management that deals with the following questions:

- At a company level, what do we want from this supplier?

- What type of behavior do we want to drive with this supplier?

- How do we want to structure the relationship with this supplier?

- How do we ensure we are aligned internally when dealing with this supplier?

- What are the appropriate tools and models for managing the interaction with this supplier?

These are crucial questions that all organizations can benefit from answering. We strongly believe that accessing the power of supplier relationships is a big untapped opportunity in so many businesses.

This Book Is Not About Procurement (At Least Not Only)

By now, it should have become clear that this book is not about procurement. Procurement, on its own, cannot answer any of the previous questions sufficiently. SRM is a cross-functional, top-management responsibility. As we'll see, the role of procurement is to orchestrate SRM and to lead the introduction of SRM in a company.

Introducing SRM in this way to a company is the key to unlocking major opportunities. In this book, we seek to shed light on how to do this. In the next chapter, we introduce the approach of TrueSRM—a fully holistic way for driving supplier behavior. In subsequent chapters, we talk about different types of supplier relationships, how to apply TrueSRM to these differentiated suppliers, and the key factors for success. We then circle back to discuss the future outlook for supplier management and how it applies to different industries. Along the way, we use a number of case studies from our own experiences as well as some from our colleagues and clients.

To illuminate and support the messages, we also reintroduce the story of the fictional characters from the novel *The CPO*, which three of us cowrote.[2]

---

[2]Schuh, Christian, Stephen Easton, Peter Scharbert, Armin Scharlach, and Michael F. Strohmer. *The CPO: Transforming Procurement in the Real World* (New York: Apress Media, 2012).

Supplier Relationship Management

A Myth?

SRM is a frequently used term that most businesspeople have heard of and recognize. It has its own Wikipedia entry. A recent search on Amazon revealed nearly 1,700 published books related to the topic. There are courses, seminars, and even Enterprise Resource Planning (ERP) system modules that are focused on it, too. Discussions with CPOs who have pursued strategic sourcing rigorously tend very quickly to move onto SRM as the "next big thing" for getting value. Procurement organizations typically have personnel and even whole departments devoted to implementing or driving SRM. People even make their careers as "SRM specialists."

Seemingly, everyone agrees that we need to have SRM.

What Is Strategic Sourcing? Strategic sourcing is a structured, systematic process for reducing the total costs of externally purchased materials, goods, and services while maintaining/improving levels of quality, service, and technology. The objective is to meet the company's business requirements from external supply markets. This is done most effectively by intervening in external supply markets in a way that takes account of the relative strength of demand power and supply power. Strategic sourcing most decidedly is not concerned explicitly with how a business manages its relationships with suppliers—that is the realm of SRM.

But, What Does It Mean?

For something that creates so much buzz, SRM is a remarkably slippery topic to put one's fingers on. The very meaning of the term is unclear.

Most people can describe some of the things that are associated with SRM practices—the "trappings" as it were. Many companies implement these trappings. It is rare now to talk to a CPO who does not have:

- Some form of understanding in place that differentiates suppliers as strategic, critical, and tactical, or other similar adjectives. This is referred to as supplier segmentation.

- Some concept of *partnership* or *collaboration* with specific suppliers—usually focused, of course, on the strategic or critical ones.

- A regime of account review meetings and performance scorecards for selected suppliers—again, usually focused on the strategic or critical ones.

The problem: Many people get hung up on these trappings as a description of what SRM is and miss the bigger picture of what actually needs to be achieved. We see countless examples of SRM programs that are focused on combinations of process design, tools, and broad concepts of supplier collaboration. All of these things have a place and can be useful, but they often miss the fundamental point that, to be effective, the behaviors of both the customer and the supplier will need to change.

The Problems

The failure to recognize this leads to a number of serious issues for businesses:

- Big investment in processes and procedures, without sufficient focus on the necessary outcomes

- A view that SRM is a "procurement topic" that "belongs" only to the CPO, to the detriment of the organization

- A silo-based approach with an inability to join up the organization's perspectives on suppliers, often leading to counterproductive messages

The net result of this is bad outcomes for both the customer and its suppliers.

Let's ponder for a moment. Think of yourself as a supplier to an organization that has gone down this road of implementing a "traditional" SRM program.

On the one hand, you may feel that this is wonderful. The business uses the language of "partnership" and probably invites you to a range of "summits" and "review" meetings where you are able to meet senior executives. Occasionally, you also get asked to fill in a "voice of the supplier" survey, which you are told is anonymous. You even get invited to give face-to-face "feedback" on how things are going. You clearly realize that you are expected to feel valued and that, possibly, your ideas for how you can contribute more to the customer's business are even valued too.

On the other hand, there is also a sense of artificiality in the air. Although you are asked to see yourself as a "partner," the deep underlying behaviors do not change. You still have to win work constantly via tenders, and you are still managed predominantly through compliance to contract. There are also more forms to fill in with respect to performance reporting and scorecards. Deep-rooted customer behavior does not seem in fact to be so very different. You pause before giving honest face-to-face feedback; deep down, you even doubt that the voice of the supplier survey that takes so much effort is really anonymous. You hesitate from being truly honest when you complete it. You also notice that the organization is still completely unable to speak with one voice on its needs and requirements. This is despite all the paraphernalia that has been put in place. You revert to form. You continue to play "divide and rule" in your dealings with the customer. You rationalize this as the only way you can possibly succeed with the customer. You may even be right.

For the customer, this whole cycle has been utterly self-defeating. A considerable amount of effort has been invested. The result has been that behaviors are unchanged, or, worse, are even more dysfunctional than they were previously. The organization still fails to manage supplier relationships in the round. Suppliers end up confused about what is wanted and do not deliver to the best of their ability. Instead, they are encouraged to "game" the organization and play divide and rule whenever they can. Suppliers who could bring crucial innovation opportunities to their customer's attention fail to do so. The customer has misapplied the "partnership" term to include nearly all big suppliers, even those who cannot really bring access to competitive advantage. The suppliers who have potential to be "true partners" have been ignored and everyone has been ground down by a need to follow "procedure." Account-review meetings have become contract-performance discussions and the segmentation matrix has not moved far beyond being a pure theoretical concept.

There is a need to break this cycle. The organization has implemented procedural SRM. It has not put in place what we describe as *TrueSRM*. TrueSRM is what is needed. We will now consider what SRM should really be about.

CASE: AUTOMAKERS IN THE MID-1990S

A case example illustrates the downside of too much, or the wrong kind of, partnership. In the mid-1990s, one of the world's most prestigious carmakers had discovered the importance of SRM for itself. The implicit understanding was that something needed to be done beyond having annual negotiations with suppliers. After analyzing what went well and what did not, the relationships with several high-end suppliers were identified as best practice.

Some of these high-end suppliers had been working with the carmaker for more than 90 years and over that period had provided many crucial innovations. The idea then was to bring all other suppliers up to the level of those key suppliers. A comprehensive SRM program was introduced and given a name that resonated well. Since many of those who were involved in the program are still around, we cannot disclose its real name in this book, but let's call it "Program Handshake" going forward.

Program Handshake was kicked off during a large supplier day with the CPO and several board members giving inspiring speeches. The new way of working was outlined to suppliers in booklets describing the new partnership type of approach. Suppliers who agreed to these principles were then called Handshake suppliers. After a very short ramp-up period, 1,500 direct material suppliers had signed up as Handshake suppliers. They represented nearly all of the carmaker's direct material spending.

The CPO lived and breathed Handshake. He was talking about Handshake wherever he went, both in internal and in external meetings. There even was an elaborate sculpture of two shaking hands on his conference table.

But the deeper he got into Handshake, the more difficult things got. The achievement of the required cost-reduction targets stalled. Whenever a supplier was challenged on cost, his response would be "This demand to cut price is against the principles of Handshake." To make matters worse, even the innovation performance dropped. The long-term, high-end suppliers continued doing what they had been doing all along, but the hundreds of other suppliers actually showed fewer innovations than prior to the introduction of Handshake.

What had happened was that suppliers in Handshake became complacent. Handshake effectively pulled the teeth out of strategic sourcing, and suppliers did not feel competitive threats anymore. Privately, supplier executives admitted overcharging the carmaker by up to 50 percent compared to other carmakers.

So, What Is TrueSRM Really About?

We take a holistic view that SRM encompasses all interactions between the customer and the supplier. At its heart, SRM:

- Drives supplier behavior

- Encompasses the relationship between two enterprises

- Enables a company to leverage its size by coordinating across divisions, functions, and hierarchies

This seemingly innocuous but broad-reaching definition means that SRM is about both top-line and bottom-line goals that encompass innovation, risk, and cost, as well as quality and responsiveness. The trappings of SRM can only be implemented and considered in terms of how they contribute to this overall goal.

A company that is applying SRM in this highly holistic way is following TrueSRM. Even today, very few organizations take this approach systematically across their full external supply base.

TrueSRM Does Not Vary by Industry/Business

Given the holistic nature of TrueSRM, one might argue that an attempt to describe how to execute it can only be meaningful on a pure industry-by-industry basis. There is some rationale in this. Clearly, the precise needs from the overall supply base will vary by industry and for each firm within the industry. Industries vary in the precise opportunity for suppliers to bring innovation, for example, or in the precise definition of risk. A chemicals company will have different objectives in these fields from a bank with quite different weightings. Different firms in the same industry will vary in things like the degree to which they outsource/insource activities. This will also have impacts on the precise needs they have from suppliers.

However, the fundamental nature of TrueSRM does not vary across industry or firms. The end requirement is the same. The precise trappings will vary but the thought process and key needs will not change. Indeed, there are major lessons to be learned by exchanging "best of breed" practices across different industries.

The Challenge

In effect, we feel that SRM today resembles strategic sourcing in the late 1980s. This was before the concept was invented and properly codified. Organizations designed specifications, issued tenders, negotiated with suppliers, and signed contracts. On occasion, they did these things very well and even achieved strong benefits from doing so. But, rather like an animal that acts from pure instinct, there was limited ability to repeat successful approaches systematically across an organization. Selecting different levers for benefit was based more on "gut feel" than on analysis or science.

The codification of strategic sourcing that started with A. T. Kearney's work in the automotive industry changed all this. Initially, a bit like with SRM today, people argued that strategic sourcing could not be applied to all industries or categories. We now know that to be false and the growth of the influence of procurement functions in the past 20 years has been strongly associated with the rollout of strategic sourcing beyond its automotive origins.

Where TrueSRM has been put in place, often in parts of businesses, the results have been very good. We are sure that, like us, most readers are familiar with excellent examples of suppliers and customers working together to drive operational improvement and create joint innovation. This is often driven by a particular working relationship that has been created, sometimes by chance. When this happens, the results are great. But it tends to happen in isolated circumstances, and is rarely systematic. Organizations that achieve these great results in one part of their supply base often still experience major issues elsewhere. The "secret sauce" is not codified.

Today's challenge for procurement is to orchestrate precisely this process by building on the great success that has already been achieved from strategic sourcing. The challenge is to manage supplier interactions on the same systematic basis that already applies to strategic sourcing. Doing so has the potential to release immeasurable value that will go far beyond mere cost saving.

This book is intended to be the guide for putting TrueSRM in place. In the next chapter, we will introduce a case study for doing this in practice.

To SRM and Beyond!

Initiating SRM in the Real World

Before we get to the core of the SRM framework we propose, let us take a look at a case study for inspiration. During the rest of this book, we will use the fictional example of Heartland Consolidated Industries to illustrate the points made in the main text. Let's say that Heartland is a global food products business headquartered in Fort Wayne, Indiana. The recently appointed CEO is a German-American named Thomas Sutter. Unusually, his prior role was as the chief procurement officer and he has owed his elevation to the success he achieved in that position. Prior to Heartland, Thomas worked for several years at Autowerke, the leading German carmaker.

Under Thomas as the CPO, the business had gone a long way toward implementing best practice procurement. He successfully imported many of the good practices that his previous company already had in place. Procurement in Heartland has become incredibly successful at meeting the perceived needs of the business, owing to its laser-like focus on reducing external costs. The external effectiveness of the function of dealing with external suppliers as well as its internal effectiveness in dealing with the wider Heartland organization has been significantly enhanced in an approach known as Holistic Procurement Transformation. As part of this approach, strategic sourcing has also been put in place systematically, and ROSMA, the overall return on supply management assets, is tracked and managed.

Laura Braida, an Italian businessperson from Milan, is the CPO now. She achieved the first key breakthrough results in the strategic sourcing program that Thomas launched when he joined Heartland. Unusual for a procurement professional, Laura has a PhD in mathematics, which she had put to good effect in the analysis that drove her strategic sourcing savings. Other key executives in our story include Garner, the CFO; Rick, the COO; and Scarlet, the CMO.

Note Astute readers may have noticed that some of the same characters appear in *The CPO* (Apress, 2012), cowritten by a number of the authors here. This book offers the backstory on these characters and the turnaround they engineered at Heartland. You can find out more information about the book at http://www.apress.com/9781430249627.

Trouble Brewing

When Thomas had been in his new role as CEO at Heartland for six months, he felt that he had fully settled into his role now. The inheritance from his predecessor, Ross, was a good one; the executive team was effective and the business largely in sound shape. Thomas now had his mind predominantly on how to grow. He felt he had largely left the cares of procurement behind, in the hands of Laura. Then, one day, Emma Jenkins, the head of investor relations, appeared in his office's anteroom and told Natalie, his executive assistant, that she had to see him as soon as possible.

Emma was immediately let into the office. Thomas was aware that Emma's role meant she often had external conversations with investors and stakeholders. Frequently, she needed to update him quickly so that he could return a call or have a conversation. However, this was different.

"Thomas, we had a call this morning from a researcher with the Corporate Responsibility Awareness Group. He says they have strong evidence that one of our packaging suppliers in Sri Lanka is using child labor. They are forcing children as young as eight to work 10 hours a day."

"Seriously?" asked Thomas.

"Yes. They wanted to give us a chance to comment. But the story is about to break. I am sure it will quickly go viral. I could not really offer a comment."

"OK. Not much you can do. I would talk to Laura so she knows. We need to find out what is happening at that supplier. I had been meaning to introduce more rigorous supplier audits when I was CPO, but it was not the number-one priority."

What became known as the Heartland Child Labor Scandal did go viral. No local laws had in fact been broken, but the adverse publicity hurt the company's stock price and considerable management attention was diverted to dealing with the issue. More importantly, Thomas saw himself as an ethical individual and genuinely wanted Heartland to operate under the same principles. He was personally upset with what had happened.

But the litany of supplier problems in what he would later call the month of mayhem was not over. Two weeks later, after the storm from the child labor scandal seemed to be passing, Thomas received an urgent e-mail from Rick Fiore, the chief operating officer, copied to Laura. A small subsupplier of a key ingredient made in Poland had suddenly stopped deliveries. The ingredient concerned was a unique flavor, which had been a major innovation for Heartland's yogurt range. It seemed that the subsupplier was having financial difficulties and one of its own suppliers, much bigger than it was, had stopped supplying essential inputs as a response to not being paid.

Clearly, Heartland had not been close enough to events in its supply chain. On further inquiry, it transpired that the company that had stopped deliveries to the Polish supplier was also a very significant direct supplier to Heartland elsewhere in its supply chain. This made the situation far more galling. The situation was rectified by the procurement, finance, and production teams working together to get the deliveries resumed in crisis management mode. Ultimately, only two days of production were lost, and the European supermarket customers saw only a blip in stock availability—but enough that several customers demanded, and received, large rebates.

Thomas now felt that perhaps there was a more systematic issue that needed resolution. He wondered if Heartland was really close enough to its suppliers. His feelings were prompted to action by receiving a third piece of news. At the end of the month, he was in his office just after 7 a.m. An early morning meeting had been scheduled with Laura to debrief on how the recent supplier problems would be avoided in future. Thomas quickly opened his iPad to check on the morning's news. To his amazement, the following headline flew across the financial section: "Calbury Consumer Industries announces launch of major new packaging innovation in conjunction with Marshfield Packaging."

The detailed article explained that the new packaging for the products kept the food fresher and tasting good for longer. The company's launch was imminent. Calbury had cofunded development and contributed expertise. Accordingly, it had exclusivity to the product for what looked like a two-year period. It looked like this would be the initiation of a more wide-ranging strategic partnership, and Thomas realized that this was a major competitive disadvantage for Heartland. To his chagrin, Marshfield was also a supplier to Heartland.

Laura walked into the office for the meeting. "What's happening?" Thomas said. "Have you seen the Calbury and Marshfield tie-up?"

"Yes," she answered. "I think this proves what we have been discussing. We need to get much more systematic in how we manage our supplier relationships, both to avoid risk and to add more value."

Laura sat down and put her laptop on the edge of Thomas's desk. "I think we need to drive SRM, Thomas. It's something I can orchestrate but it really needs to be owned more broadly." She opened up her laptop and said, "I have a short slide deck. Do you have a minute to . . . ?"

Thomas stopped her. "Please, Laura, not an SRM program." He said "program" very slowly and dwelled over the syllables. "SRM programs rarely achieve much," he said. "I saw all this at Autowerke. They were just a way to get more discounts, really."

She agreed. "Most CPOs have done 'something' they label as SRM but without a consistent, compelling view on the business objective of SRM and what should be included in a SRM capability. As a result, many of these companies fail to fully channel the energy of their supply base for competitive advantage. What we need is what I would call TrueSRM as opposed to only a set of processes and procedures."

Despite the dramas of the past couple of weeks, Laura clearly saw an opportunity. She envisioned that procurement would become far more of a strategic function for the business than it currently was. She explained that this would need to be achieved by working closely with the executives to collectively make progress in the company's three to five year strategic plan with a comprehensive SRM capability aimed at building a sustainable competitive advantage. Done that way, she said, SRM would work.

Rather than spell out all the details of the program, Laura had a simple "ask" for Thomas. She wanted to run workshops with the executive team to chart the journey toward SRM.

"Thomas, I can orchestrate SRM. But if I try to determine everything within procurement, it won't work."

"What will the workshops look like?" asked Thomas.

"The objective would be to come up with answers to five beautifully simple questions."

She pointed to a slide on her screen that read: "What is SRM? Why do SRM? Why do SRM now? What does it take to build a leading SRM capability? What is the best way to get started?"

Thomas relented. "OK, Laura, let's give it a go."

But she had one further request: "Thomas, you need to be the executive sponsor. This must be owned from the top. It is simply too important not to be."

Thomas was a little concerned that this would potentially pull him back into procurement and overshadow Laura's role. However, he saw the logic. The three issues of the month of mayhem really were a mission critical for the business. If Heartland could head off such debacles . . . .

He agreed. Over the following couple of weeks, a series of workshops addressed Laura's five questions one by one. Thomas attended each session and Laura chaired them. Rick, the COO; Garner, the CFO; and Scarlet, the CMO, were also present. Each workshop addressed one question and was scheduled to last one-and-a-half hours at the end of the day—a good moment for reflective discussion in the Heartland culture. Thought was given to just holding a single all-day session to attack all five questions. However, it was felt that shorter sessions over a period with the opportunity for participants to reflect would achieve a much better outcome. It would also make scheduling easier.

The First Workshop

On a Tuesday afternoon at 5:00 p.m., all of the executives filed into a meeting room to tackle the first question, What is SRM?

Laura started the session: "Maybe the best way to start this," she said, "is if we all give an initial view of what we think SRM is." This seemingly innocuous question actually turned out to be very hard to answer. There were quite different views in the room.

Garner started: "For me, it is about making sure that suppliers perform and do not let us down." Scarlet nodded in agreement and added, "It's also about making sure that we mitigate any risks we have from external suppliers." The child labor issue in Sri Lanka was still very much on her mind, but she did not want to refer to it directly; the experience had been too painful for all concerned.

"OK," said Laura. "So, SRM needs to include performance and risk management." She captured those points on the whiteboard.

"What you do with suppliers somehow needs to be differentiated too," said Rick. "We would not want to manage performance and risk as rigorously for a stationery supplier as we would for a supplier from which we get core ingredients."

Laura interjected: "This is what in procurement we talk about as segmentation of the supply base. We use that as a basis to treat different types of suppliers differently." She wrote "Supplier segmentation" on the whiteboard.

Thomas now spoke up: "It's also about making sure that we are coordinated. We need to be able to speak as a single voice to suppliers. That way, they know where they stand and no supplier will be tempted to play "divide and rule" with us. It's hard to do given that we are big and global, but that understanding must be part of this."

They all nodded. Laura noted the point. They now had three definitions on the whiteboard:

—Performance and risk management

—Supplier segmentation

—Coordinated supplier communication across all business units, functions, and hierarchy levels.

"Is that all?" asked Laura.

"No," said Scarlet. "Those are good foundations. But I think it is really about more than that. I want to work with suppliers to get more out of the relationships. That goes beyond pure performance management or making sure the contract is delivered. For example, from the creative agency I want the absolute A Team to give us the best marketing ideas that we can develop. I want more value. I want innovation."

"Do you want innovation from every supplier?" inquired Laura.

"Well, I suppose the politically correct answer is to say yes," said Scarlet. "But, in reality, as a business, it is not always so critical to get that from every supplier, nor is it a realistic desire. From our suppliers of printed materials, I really just need on-time delivery and a hardworking response to our specifications each time."

"So, there are strategic elements to SRM that do not apply to every supplier," said Laura.

"When we talk about suppliers who are really valuable," said Thomas, "we will also be thinking about how we can work with them to create ecosystems that give us a competitive advantage. But that will be with a handful of suppliers at most, I would say."

"So, the strategic elements only apply to select suppliers based on the segmentation we just discussed," said Laura. Then, she wrote on the whiteboard:

—Improvement initiatives that go beyond current contractual commitments

—Value maximization across the ecosystem

"We have five key points," she said. "Three foundational aspects apply to all suppliers and then these more strategic needs apply to a smaller number of select suppliers only." She paused and then said: "We still do not have an overarching definition of SRM though, do we? Do we need one?"

"I think it would help," said Rick.

Thomas intervened again: "I think we are saying that SRM should encompass all interactions with suppliers. This includes foundational elements that are applicable to all suppliers and the strategic elements that are applicable to select suppliers."

That seemed to work for them. There was general nodding. Laura said, "Well, now we know what SRM is. On Thursday, we will agree why we need to do it!"

The Second Workshop

The group reconvened at the same time two days later to answer the question, Why should we pursue SRM?

"You know," remarked Thomas, "this is not such a simple question to answer actually."

"I know," said Laura. "The entire culture of procurement is focused on savings. Everybody understands that the reason to do strategic sourcing is to receive better value for your money. When they say that, they really mean cut costs and get savings."

"As the CFO, I have to say that there is nothing wrong with savings, as long as they are real," Garner pointed out.

"I like savings too," said Laura with a smile. "But, SRM is a much broader topic. I am not so sure we all have the same objectives in mind."

Scarlet then jumped in. "Supplier management is not really something that procurement does, Laura. To the extent that it happens, it is we in the business who do it."

"SRM is delegated to users," said Laura. "I agree with you."

"I am not sure I would use the word *delegated*," commented Scarlet. "It implies that there is some conscious choice or mandate that is possessed by procurement in the first place."

"Point taken," said Laura. "I think we can agree on the following: While procurement leads sourcing efforts and negotiates the contracts that reduce unit price, it is the users that actually manage the day-to-day and strategic aspects of the supplier relationship and many times they do not even include procurement in decisions. As a result, suppliers maintain and coordinate an extensive network of interactions and personal contacts with us while the company lacks transparency on the overall relationship. The situation is not optimal, is it?"

"That's right," Thomas affirmed.

Some debate ensued over what exactly made sense to do. Rick felt that the individual functions should provide better transparency on day-to-day supplier compliance with supplier scorecards.

Scarlet wanted to drive value beyond compliance and experiment with supplier innovation conferences and executive sponsors. "I think we should hold a big supplier summit and even give awards as a way to build enthusiasm," she said. Thomas and Laura exchanged glances.

"That's a classic marketing approach, Scarlet," Thomas said with a smile to show that he understood her perspective. "I'm sure there is a place for that, but we need to address the key question of why we should do this!"

"You prompt an idea though, Scarlet," added Laura. "We do want excitement from our key suppliers. This needs to be bold. SRM is the opportunity for us to channel the energy of our supply base for competitive advantage."

Scarlet interjected: "Yes. SRM should be driven by creating a sustainable competitive advantage through the pursuit of value beyond cost reduction—growth and innovation, risk management, capital optimization, and so on."

"And cost, don't forget cost," said Garner.

"We won't forget that, my friend," responded Thomas. "But, the ultimate prize from SRM is really to team with select suppliers and build a competitively advantaged ecosystem, isn't it? That's what we want to do as a business, surely. Cost reduction only gets us so far. Right?"

There was nodding, even from Garner, who said, "Actually, we are about to enter our five-year strategic planning cycle again. SRM needs to be part of that."

"You are right," said Thomas. "SRM really requires a focus on enabling our five-year plan. SRM can contribute to this year's business plan, but the primary payoff is longer term. I think we all agree?"

There was general nodding around the table.

"Tomorrow, we will talk about why we need to do this now," concluded Laura, "instead of waiting."

The Third Workshop

The third question—of why Heartland needs to institute SRM now—was relatively easy for the group to answer.

Laura opened the discussion: "We have sourced our supply base lots of times now. We know which suppliers are best suited for the key areas of spending. Constant threats to switch suppliers are losing their credibility."

"I agree," said Rick. "In fact, a significant portion of the supply base is so entrenched in our business models that there are few viable alternatives anyway."

"I think we all know that a sole focus on cost reduction is not sufficient to meet the dynamics of today's global economy," offered Thomas. "I've been thinking about this," he said as he consulted some notes. He then quickly wrote the following summaries of key macro-economic points on the whiteboard:

—Changing growth imperatives: evolving demographics and consumption, increased commoditization

—An increased demand for sustainability: avoiding depletion of natural resources, focus on sustainable designs

—Higher levels of risk: elevated financial volatility, rising commodity costs

—Tighter regulation: changing role of government, more regulations

At this point, Thomas paused and looked down again at his notes. He said, "Oh yes, and let's not forget that cost does not go away as an objective either." He then wrote:

—Continued pressure on cost: new paradigms, realignment of global supply chain

He continued speaking. "But, let's not forget the month of mayhem we just had. The issues we had were all about innovation and risk management. They were supplier issues. I do not want to have a repeat of that. I think that is why we need to do this now, and not wait!"

"Yes, we need to get on with it," agreed Garner.

"Right," said Scarlet. "We need a supplier-centric approach to value beyond cost reduction. We need to start it now."

Laura ended with, "OK, next week, we tackle the remaining questions. I hope that is soon enough for us all."

The Fourth Workshop

The group reconvened at 5:00 p.m. on Monday. Laura introduced the session: "We have defined what SRM is, why we need it, and why we need to implement it as fast as we can. Today we need to discuss this question, What does it take to build a leading SRM capability?"

"I think that is tricky," said Thomas.

"Yes," agreed Laura. "Today, in all the companies that I have reached out to for best practice comparisons, SRM is severely underdeveloped versus strategic sourcing. Specifically, in none of them is SRM established as a robust and repeatable process consistently deployed across the enterprise. They are even prepared to admit that, and as you know we are all quite proud and hate to admit failings externally!"

There was then quite a bit of discussion about how difficult it would be to implement SRM. A little way into the conversation, Rick spoke up: "I have been thinking about this. Successful SRM really requires the development of an integrated, comprehensive operating model that is focused on driving value. This 'form follows function' operating model needs to include repeatable management processes, enabling tools, key metrics, inclusive governance, new people skills, and supporting organizational structures that are guided by a set of commonly understood principles."

"I think that is right," said Laura. The others nodded.

Rick continued: "At a high level, this operating model includes a number of elements." He then jotted the following elements on the whiteboard:

—Processes: compliance management, segmentation, collaboration

—Tools: scorecards, comprehensive intercompany trade-flow maps

—Metrics and incentives: value measurement and gain sharing

—Governance: interlocking cross-enterprise executive sponsors, committees

—Talent: people skilled in collaborative problem solving and communications

—Organizational structure: focused departments positioned to work in a complex environment

There was general agreement on the points.

"I do not want to push back on our urgency to get this done and in place," Rick said. "But, my sense is that there will be quite a lot of work involved. We do not have all the capability we need. We need to build it and/or acquire it."

"You are right," agreed Laura.

Thomas chimed in: "I could certainly see you needing to do a lot more to put the right capability in place within procurement to orchestrate this."

Laura responded, "Yes. I guess that takes us on to our final question, too: What is the best way to get started? We talk about that on Wednesday."

The Fifth Workshop

"How do we get started?" was Garner's opening statement the next time the group met. "That is a really tough question. It seems to me that we are trailblazing. There are so few best practice examples to learn from. It is never easy."

"I think we need to learn from other initiatives we have already deployed across Heartland," Thomas offered. "Goes without saying really, but we also need to be pragmatic."

"When we put in place the global marketing operating model across all our businesses, we had a similar challenge," commented Scarlet. "We needed to change the way we were doing things, be more consistent but still allow for quick and decisive decision making on the frontline."

"It worked well," said Rick.

Scarlet continued. "That would mean we need to set up a joint task force to establish a common-core SRM capability that will serve as a guideline for the whole of Heartland. Individual businesses and functions will then be allowed to tailor this core SRM capability to their situation while maintaining the ability to speak to suppliers with a common voice."

"Yes," said Laura. "We then need to do this in a 'test and learn' mindset that measures and communicates value realized. As we proceed, we need to learn the lessons and get better."

"I agree," said Thomas.

"I will start to work up a plan," said Laura. "This has been a very helpful series of meetings. I suggest we review it at our executive meeting this coming Monday."

Getting to TrueSRM

The team left the room. Laura then approached Thomas, who asked her, "Did that achieve your objectives?"

"I think so," she said. "But there is one issue. Even after all this, I think that there is still a missing ingredient."

"I think so too," said Thomas. "It's great that we have alignment on all these questions, but I'm not sure we are really there yet either. Our whole problem with this started because we have not been managing suppliers properly. For that, one size really does not fit all. I have seen traditional segmentation approaches and, for me, these really never work. They are never applied properly either. What do you think?"

Laura responded, "I think we need to take a much more effective approach. We need to have a genuinely differentiated strategy for managing our interactions holistically with suppliers. That is what I really see as living and breathing TrueSRM. I have some ideas . . . ."

Key to a Profitable Future

Right now, Heartland is at the stage where it realizes it needs to manage supplier interactions more effectively and more comprehensively across its business. It also needs to do this sooner rather than later; there is a genuine imperative. At the very least, the CEO does not want to endure another month of mayhem.

Although the Heartland case is fictional, it mirrors real-life experiences that we have had with SRM. We have worked extensively with clients who have implemented strategic sourcing across their businesses, and who are adept at negotiating to achieve "savings." However, these clients were missing the "secret sauce" of how to manage supplier relationships effectively to achieve wider objectives associated with innovation, sustainability, and risk management. We developed and implemented TrueSRM with clients precisely to address these needs that are highlighted in the Heartland experience.

In the next chapter, we will address the question that Laura and Thomas have left us with—how to effectively put TrueSRM in place. We will describe the key that is needed to unlock "the genuinely differentiated approach to managing our interactions holistically with suppliers," which is the idea Thomas is searching for. This is where interaction models enter our story.

Introducing Supplier Interaction Models

The Framework for SRM Success

One of the core ambitions we had when we developed the TrueSRM program was to develop a practical framework that actually worked. Too many prior SRM initiatives got stuck at a philosophical level that let companies believe things like the idea that they should partner with all suppliers. Chapter 2 discussed other SRM initiatives that have focused fully on processes and IT systems that manage who is talking to which supplier about what. While this aspect of the system might be useful, it falls short of the true potential in SRM.

The workable framework we aspired to develop aims at a lot more than merely suggesting partnerships or managing processes. As we suggested, in our view, SRM is ultimately about motivating suppliers to behave in ways that will meet a company's needs.

With this objective in mind, two requirements for the framework emerged:

- It needs to separate those suppliers that really matter from the overwhelming number of suppliers a company usually has.

- It needs to provide specific recommendations on how to interact with suppliers that fall into its different areas.

In order to separate the suppliers that really matter from the others, we looked into dimensions that allow us to gauge what a supplier means to a company. This process was fairly straightforward. We essentially said that it is important to take into consideration the supplier's current performance and the supplier's strategic potential. With this, we had the two axes of the SRM framework.

Bringing the framework to life was more challenging. The first question to clarify was whether we would propose distinct models or an unlimited number of shades of grey. Our 2008 book, *The Purchasing Chessboard*, suggested shades of grey. In this model, a category gets mapped onto the chessboard and then the 64 methods that are in the general area of the category get evaluated for their relevance to the specific category. Since the chessboard (Figure 4-1) is mainly used by specialists dealing with that specific category, this ambiguity made a lot of sense. For further information on the Purchasing Chessboard, see http://www.purchasingchessboard.com.

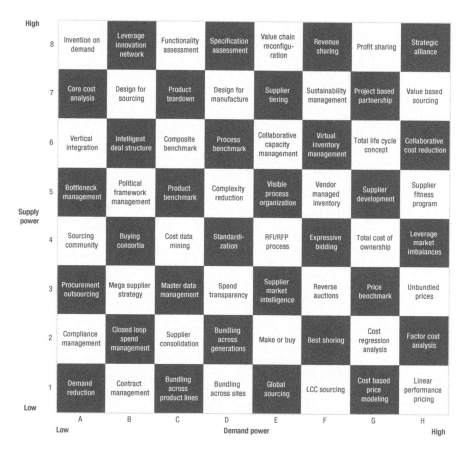

Figure 4-1. The Purchasing Chessboard

With SRM, we are dealing with a very different environment. The SRM framework will be applied by senior executives from different functional areas. It therefore needs distinct models that are easy to use. After several iterations, we settled on a three-by-three logic with nine distinct supplier interaction models. While it is not trivial to remember nine different models and their position relative to each other, we found it just at the limit of being doable. After a couple of days of practice, senior executives in the pilot companies we worked with got comfortable with the nine interaction models and started using them in a natural way.

This chapter provides a high-level introduction to the two axes of the framework and the nine interaction models (see Figure 4-2).

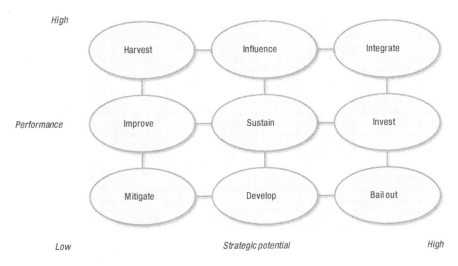

Figure 4-2. The TrueSRM framework

Performance Axis

There are a number of supplier-performance variables that potentially matter to a customer. At the highest aggregation level, these include time (e.g., on-time, in-full deliveries); cost (e.g., savings vs. the previous period); and quality (e.g., number of implemented improvement ideas in the period).

On a closer look, most systems used to measure the performance of suppliers are not really ideal. Often, the systems are very complex, measuring hundreds of performance indicators, and nobody can explain exactly why their specific indicators and not others are in place. Also, we have observed output factors, like savings performance, and input factors, like the excellence of engineering processes being merged together. Further, weighing factors doesn't increase the effectiveness of these performance measurement systems.

Then there is the human factor. Different evaluators tend to interpret performance indicators differently and also look at suppliers differently. We have seen wildly fluctuating supplier performance that turned out to be driven not by the supplier's actual performance but by the variance in people conducting the performance appraisal.

While existing supplier performance measurement systems need to be taken with a grain of salt, they at least provide a starting point for populating the performance axis of the SRM framework. In an ideal world, an SRM initiative might start with overhauling supplier performance management.

Each of the functions having interfaces with a supplier would come up with a very limited set of performance indicators. These would then be consolidated into a lean and effective performance indicator structure that would be shared with suppliers.

It is tempting to go down this avenue, but we would not recommend it. Many SRM initiatives have gone wrong doing exactly that. Supplier performance indicators can become very emotional topics that can easily be debated hotly over many months. So, our recommendation is to work with whatever you have today and leave fixing supplier performance measurement for a later point in time.

The real challenge is to make the existing performance measurement meaningful. This can be done most effectively by borrowing from an HR department. Employee performance management processes are typically burdened by an inflation of too many excellent ratings. The way of HR people to deal with this is to ask for forced rankings of employees. In essence, the managers of two excellent employees will be asked to agree on which of the two employees is even more excellent than the other. We propose deploying the same principle for populating the performance axis of the TrueSRM framework.

Here's how it might work: Initially, you would tap into the available supplier performance reports. You would then aggregate these reports across business units on a supplier level. If all business units are similar in size, no weighing is necessary. If there is a substantial difference in size and if business units do have significantly different requirements, appropriate weighing approaches should be introduced. This weighing could simply be based on the relative revenue of different businesses. But one might feel that this would lead suppliers to neglect the smaller businesses. This would be especially counterproductive if the smaller businesses are high growth and consequently need high-performing suppliers to support that growth. In that case, one could base the weighing on a pure arithmetic average of the scores in different businesses. Or, one may still base the initial weighing on relative revenue but then make adjustments for different growth prospects.

You would then calibrate the aggregated performance reports to achieve a normal distribution, or bell curve, over the performance axis. With this normal distribution, 5 percent of suppliers would fall into the high-performance category, another 5 percent would fall into low performance, and the remaining 90 percent of suppliers would fall into the medium performance category.

If you are reading closely, you see where this is going. In TrueSRM, we want to focus the company's top management attention and resources on those suppliers that really matter. And the suppliers that matter are the top performers and the underperformers.

Top performers matter because they are the suppliers that have the most chance of helping the company shape its future. Not all top performers will be able to help shape the company's future, and it is particularly hard to see that a supplier whose performance is not excellent will be able to do so.

Underperformers also matter because they drag the entire company down. They tie up valuable resources used fixing the delivery, cost, and quality issues they cause. Something needs to be done about underperformers.

The vast majority of suppliers in the middle may matter from a different perspective. But as long as we have untapped potential with high-performing suppliers, and unresolved issues with low-performing suppliers, they will not be the focus of attention. This is why it is usually counterproductive to start by overhauling and refining to the nth degree the approach to supplier performance measurement. The approach needs to be robust enough to enable the high performers and low performers to be triaged. It does not need to enable the 63rd percentile to be distinguished from the 62nd percentile, particularly given that suppliers provide different goods and services in any case.

Strategic Potential Axis

We have seen that populating the performance axis is tricky even when we do have data we can build on. Populating the strategic potential axis is far more difficult. Most companies do not have any established mechanisms to gauge the strategic potential of a supplier. Even worse, many companies are using the term "partner" in an inflationary way. Any high-performing supplier, or just a big one, will often be labeled as partner or even strategic partner.

While we cautioned about rebuilding the supplier performance evaluation system of a company when embarking on the SRM journey, we encourage doing just that for the strategic potential axis. There cannot be any TrueSRM as long as the key decision makers of the company are not aligned on what makes a supplier strategically important.

When we say strategic potential, we mean the relevance the supplier can have in relation to the execution of the company's strategy. A supplier with high strategic potential should hold the key to a competitive advantage for the company. This competitive advantage might not yet be realized today because either the company has not yet understood how to tap into the supplier's potential or because the supplier's current performance blurs the view on the strategic potential.

The high-level strategic potential of a supplier can be measured across a number of indicators:

- *Growth*: Does the supplier offer capabilities that could improve the company's value proposition for existing customers or generate sales with new customers? Examples would be wide geographic reach of the supplier or an excellent understanding of customer needs.

- *Innovation*: Does the supplier own or propose new technologies that could lead to breakthrough for the company's products and services? Examples would be a supplier that has developed critical patents or conducted strategic mergers and acquisitions.

- *Scope*: Is the supplier relevant for the company across most business units? An example of such a supplier would be a true portfolio player that supports the company by supplying all of its divisions.

- *Collaboration*: Does the supplier demonstrate the right mindset in working with the company across different functional areas? An example would be a supplier that leverages its critical capabilities in an effective way.

For the introduction of the strategic potential axis, we suggest a fairly provocative approach. In contrast to the often inflationary use of the terms *strategic* and *partner*, in our view, the default strategic potential of a supplier should be low. We strongly believe that at least 90 percent of suppliers have very limited strategic potential to a company.

While populating the performance axis of the SRM framework is done in a bottom-up way, for the strategic potential axis we suggest doing it with a top-down approach. Top management should get together and determine the suppliers that have high or medium strategic potential. Overall, we would expect to find 2 percent of suppliers at most to have high strategic potential and 8 percent of suppliers to have medium strategic potential. In most cases, the high-potential strategic suppliers should amount to only a couple of handfuls.

The Framework

Looking at the overall picture in Figure 4-3, a pattern begins to emerge. Most suppliers will be center left in the portfolio, which means that they have average performance and are in mature business relationships. A limited number of suppliers will reside in the "interesting areas" at the corners of the portfolio. This leads to the question of how to interact with these suppliers.

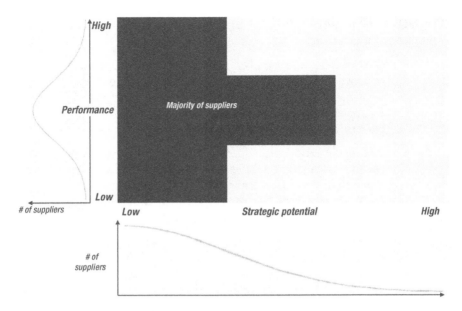

Figure 4-3. The expected distribution of suppliers

Regardless of industry, company size, or a dozen other factors, suppliers tend to fall into three distinct camps: There are those in the "critical cluster" that can contribute to competitive advantage, with some nurturing of the relationship. There are the "ordinaries" that can provide needed but common products or services that could be purchased from many other sources. And then there are those "problematic" ones that have been useful sources of supply but pose serious problems that need to be fixed or the supplier replaced.

Managing supplier relationships is nothing new, of course. What is new is our system for recognizing what characterizes a supplier in relation to a company's unique business objectives. What is the core nature of the relationship? How can it better serve the company's success? What do the suppliers themselves want? And how do we communicate with them, both in terms of where they stand now and where we want them to be in the future? This last point is especially pertinent because supplier relationships are rarely structured in a way that guides internal conversations and planning, or allows for communication in actionable terms.

Identifying individual formulas or models that together characterize TrueSRM is the premise that drove the project team to develop nine ways to interact with suppliers. Each model gets to the heart of what makes the most common and effective supplier relationships tick while establishing expectations for what each relationship is capable of and laying the groundwork for mutual success. While there is no substitute for classic sourcing or the proficiency of our Purchasing Chessboard, our supplier relationship management approach is designed to identify and support those relationships that pose the greatest return on investment while considering the limited time constraints of many CPOs.

The Nine Relationships

Figure 4-4 introduces the nine supplier relationship models in detail:

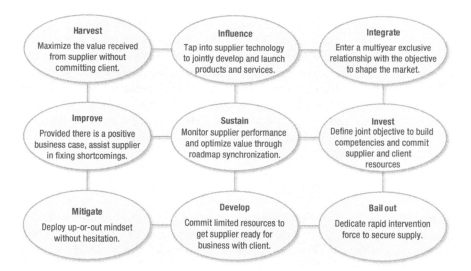

Figure 4-4. Nine interaction models

Critical Cluster: The Relationships to Nurture

The first category under our microscope, the critical cluster, includes the three types of suppliers that offer the most promise. Whether they are the vendors that already have a great relationship with you, or the ones that clearly could have one with a little work, these relationships are the valuable few that are worth time and attention.

Integrate: Worthy of Commitment

In this box, we find the Integrate model, where the two organizations have goals that are genuinely integrated and they work together as partners. To put it colloquially, this is a partnership with a capital "P". Although an often-overused term in business, this type of true partnership is rare and is based on a multiyear, differentiated, and comprehensive relationship between you and your supplier to build an ecosystem that shapes the market. The supplier chosen for this model should be in your sweet spot: its performance needs to be flawless, and it needs to hold the key to making you a formidable competitor by creating opportunities to grow revenues and profits while jointly shaping or reshaping the industry.

Influence: Joint Development of New Offerings

Suppliers that fit the Influence model in this box deliver nearly perfect products or services. What sets them apart is that they offer the potential for innovation by working with you to jointly develop new products or services. This factor shapes your relationship with them. These suppliers often dominate an industry, as they are the crucial few that a company and its competitors rely on. In turn, they do not favor any one customer, and in the case of monopolistic suppliers, are required by law not to do so. The downside, of course, is that it is nearly impossible to outpace your competition by working with these suppliers. What's more, mismanage this relationship and you could alienate these suppliers enough that you fall behind competitors that may be better at handling their relationship with the same supplier.

Invest: Promise of Capability

Does your company have suppliers that offer great ideas and innovations but then stumble in some basic areas, such as providing continuous supply or consistent quality? Those suppliers fall into the Invest model. A great future can be had with these suppliers—as they ultimately could reach Integrate status—but their potential for this rests on the relationship you build with them now and the extent to which they respond. Ideally, an Invest supplier will aspire to Integrate status and will invest with you in building capabilities to achieve this title. Here, we recommend nurturing the relationship by investing time, money, and resources in developing the supplier's capabilities to meet your needs. The best candidates will make capability building a top priority. Be forewarned, however, that some suppliers may spurn the help, believing that you are attempting to make them "captive" and cut them off from wider market opportunities.

Ordinaries: The Widget Providers

While the three supplier types that fall into the ordinary camp are generally more numerous, don't let their average status fool you. There is strength in numbers here. With more of these dime-a-dozen suppliers in your fold, having a keen understanding of what makes these relationships tick, and a simple set of tools for maintaining or incrementally improving their performance, can have sizeable positive results for you.

Harvest: Highly Productive But Still Needs Cultivating

The Harvest model represents a well-functioning position for both parties. The company receives exactly the type of products or services it needs from the supplier. These things are nearly perfect, in fact, and support the company's competitiveness. For you and the supplier, this relationship is virtually hassle-free and ties up few resources. It may seem to function on its own, and that's exactly where both parties need to focus. Complacency should be the red flag here. Great performance could be mistaken for a great partnership. We recommend not using the term "partner" loosely, because it can lead to assumptions that nothing needs to be changed. Low investment of resources can communicate that you don't overtly value this relationship and that if the supplier falters, it could be dropped. The Harvest supplier's vulnerability, then, and the absence of discussion about maintaining performance, can create tension that negatively influences interactions between the parties.

Sustain: Worthy of Continuous Improvement

You probably work with a number of Sustain suppliers. Their performance is average, but aspects of this type of relationship place it above the ones you have with most suppliers, usually because you need these relationships to endure. They do not need major fixes or warrant significant investment. However, undertaking incremental improvement to capture more value and move performance toward world-class levels can usually benefit you.

Improve: Shortcomings Need to Be Addressed

The majority of your suppliers are likely to fit in the Improve category. They perform at a level similar to that of a Sustain supplier, but with shortcomings. The key difference is that should they fail—especially repeatedly—you would be more likely to replace them than you would a faltering Sustain supplier. The Improve relationship can feel unstable for both you and the supplier as a result. Instead, to profit from the relationship you will learn to turn the unknowns into opportunities by helping the Improve supplier to raise performance and move toward Harvest status.

Problematic Suppliers: The Serious Fixes

Rather than rue the day you hired certain suppliers that have become problematic, take a close look at what has gone wrong and learn from everyone's mistakes. Indeed, this is the time to contain the damage. It's also a great opportunity to repair relationships that warrant the investment, or at least keep the lines of communication open should you both go your separate ways but later find that things look better.

Mitigate: Need to Be Disengaged on Good Terms

Sometimes, it just doesn't work out. The Mitigate supplier has significant ongoing issues with delivery, cost, or quality, for example, and it's time to replace this source with one that is more promising. The risks and consequences of doing this then need to be mitigated. Relationships that reach the Mitigate stage are easy to transition out of when the failing supplier is small or the business is simply structured. But when there are multiple lines of business, numerous product segments, or big outsourcing agreements with a long-term supplier, replacement becomes a challenge. Paradoxically, the quality of this relationship—even though it is ending—is one of the most important supplier interactions to maintain at a level of openness and clarity while you are still working together.

Develop: Candidates for the Ideal Source

To establish a competitive advantage and operational benefits where none currently exist, consider building a Develop relationship with a supplier whose current performance is poor and needs to be addressed. This should be a hand-selected vendor with lots of potential for working closely with you to identify opportunities across its value chain and yours. Reach out to your in-house cross-functional teams to identify viable candidates that are currently not ready for prime time but have the basic potential to become star suppliers. There are numerous examples of Develop suppliers that become key sources in well-managed relationships that last for years. Consider, for example, the many manufacturers that nurture low-cost country suppliers, providing technology or engineering assistance to get them up to speed as component suppliers.

Bail Out: Stepping In Is Necessary

A major supplier commits an egregious error or a chronic problem suddenly requires triage. This is the abrupt formation of the Bail Out relationship. The situation can significantly jeopardize business by threatening supply.

The immediate goal is to stabilize the performance of the supplier, whose reaction will be hard to predict. Long term, look to learn from the problem to avoid future bail outs with this supplier. It may seem counterintuitive, but this is a relationship that will likely be maintained, particularly with important suppliers. The Bail Out relationship itself should be brief, rarely occur, and be regarded as a temporary step toward improving the overall supplier relationship.

Heartland Develops TrueSRM

Meanwhile, back at Heartland Industries, Thomas and Laura were grappling with their recognition that they needed an approach for TrueSRM.

After her conversation with Thomas following the final workshop, Laura went back to her office and pondered the situation. She realized that, as CEO, Thomas did not want to be concerned with all the details of every supplier. Of course. That was a given. As CPO, she herself could not be concerned with every supplier. Heartland had several thousand suppliers globally, and this was unlikely to change radically. She also pondered what Thomas had meant by "managing our interactions holistically with suppliers." The word *holistically* caused her to pause. She felt that it made sense. Heartland needed to set up SRM in a way that enabled it to orchestrate all dimensions of a supplier relationship—performance, cost, behaviors, risk, and so forth. But this had to be tailored to the specifics of the relationship. Otherwise, this would be far too unwieldy and resource intensive for the business to execute. There needed to be some form of differentiation that the business could implement.

Laura had seen segmentation approaches before, but she had not seen one that really provided a basis for managing interactions in the differentiated way that she sought. One approach that she had seen talked about had you identify "strategic," "core," and "noncore" suppliers. This had always led to lots of debate about what exactly a strategic supplier was. Previously, she had seen the word strategic used as a proxy for "large," which missed the point. Marshfield, which had just tied up with Calbury Industries, was not a particularly large organization.

Laura sensed that many of the most valuable suppliers, who could bring exclusive innovation, were indeed likely to be small, entrepreneurial, and lacking "pedigree." She thought of digital marketing, for example, as an area that classic advertising agencies were still grappling with. Heartland might prefer not to deal with the established players at all in this space and instead bypass them. "Young start-ups might just be able to bring what the business needs as our suppliers," she mused. "They might not be operationally so robust, though." Clearly, there is a big distinction to draw between current performance and strategic potential.

"Conversely, some suppliers perform well but lack strategic potential," she thought. "Best not to spend too much time on them." She wondered about what to call them. "Well, they certainly are not particularly special suppliers. They are actually quite ordinary, really. Maybe then we should call these 'Ordinaries.' Most of our suppliers belong in this camp." Others, she knew, perform well and have great strategic potential. Marshfield might have belonged in this camp. These are suppliers that need strong attention—including personal attention from Thomas. They are far more special. "Probably better not to call them special, though. They are critical to the business." She now had a name for them. "That's it—these are the 'Critical Cluster.' Then, there are other suppliers who basically give us problems. That's an easy name. They are the 'Problematic Suppliers,' who have either performance issues, limited strategic potential, or both. Big danger if we spend too much time on these suppliers. Although the ones with poor performance but strong strategic potential might be worthy of being nurtured. We would need to make our bets carefully."

Laura really felt she had made progress in how to work through to TrueSRM. It was close to the end of the day now. She got her Stylus out and started to draw on her iPad. She labeled the vertical axis "Performance" and the horizontal axis "Strategic Potential." [Figure 4-5.] She then drew the three clusters. She placed the Critical Cluster on the top right, Problematic Suppliers horizontally across the bottom, and Ordinaries to fill the rest of the screen. She decided to go back to see Thomas. "Time for action," she muttered under her breath as she left her office.

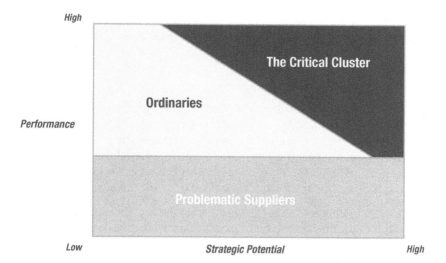

Figure 4-5. The three clusters

Thomas's office door was wide open and Laura walked in. She showed him what she had done on her iPad and emphasized how it would help them to prioritize executive effort.

"So we focus on how well they perform now versus their potential value. Makes sense," he mused. "I just wonder whether three clusters is really granular enough to be actionable."

"You may be right," said Laura. "Shall we sketch it on the whiteboard and think about it?"

Thomas nodded. Laura drew the two axes. She added the three clusters. They focused first on the top right-hand corner.

"At the very top right will be the closest relationships," said Thomas. "That's obvious."

"The true partnerships," added Laura.

"Yes," Thomas agreed. "But, I am not sure we should use the P word. It's so overused that I think it is often meaningless. These are really situations where we want to achieve some close form of integration between our business and theirs. Maybe we call these Integrate."

"Right," Laura replied. "The bottom-left corner is easy too. That is where we want to get out of an unsatisfactory relationship without breaking too much china. So, let's just call it Mitigate. The extremities are probably the easiest ones. What about the top left?"

"That's interesting," said Thomas. "A high-performing supplier where we do not really value the strategic potential. It's the sort of supplier we sometimes see in noncore categories. They can be really good at what they do, but we'd only notice if they suddenly stopped. This is the type of relationship where we just sit back and harvest the good work they do. Let's call these Harvest."

"Great," remarked Laura. "Bottom right are the suppliers we value a lot, but their current performance is a big issue and can stop us shipping product. These are the situations where we need to step in ourselves to fix things or to bail the supplier out. So, let's call these Bail Out."

"I agree," Thomas replied. "What about the middle of the board? That feels like the next logical place to go. In the very middle, we have relationships that we value. But, they have only average or so-so performance. We probably need to maintain or sustain these relationships, but they are not overly exciting for us."

"So, we can call them Sustain," suggested Laura.

Five interaction models had now been created.

"Now, for the more challenging ones between the extremes," proceeded Thomas. "Let's start top middle. These are strong suppliers that we need to be successful, but that we will probably never be in a position to integrate with."

Laura interjected. "In these cases, our aim should probably be to influence them to provide innovation on a limited scale."

"So maybe we should call these Influence," proposed Thomas. "What about the right middle?"

"There we have middling performance but high strategic potential. So, perhaps these are suppliers where we may need to establish some form of joint action or investment with to create something special between us. It could be a new capability that is greater than either of us already has, or a new facility for example. Perhaps we call that Invest," suggested Laura.

"That works," said Thomas. "Good, seven models defined. What about the bottom middle?"

"Poor performance, reasonable relationship value. Sounds like these are suppliers we want to keep but something needs to happen so they can meet our performance needs. We probably need to devote some effort to help that happen, but without overdoing things."

"So we can call these Develop then. One more left. Middle left."

"Low relationship value and middling performance," was Laura's assessment. "No obvious reason why we would invest much in such a relationship. These are suppliers where we need them to step up more if they are to continue with us. They need to do better."

"We can call them Improve," Thomas suggested. "Great, we have a 3 x 3 matrix. Consultants usually do 2 x 2. We have gone one better," he joked. "Where do you think most suppliers sit in this framework, Laura?"

"Oh, I think mainly toward the left. There will be very few in the top right. But, the top right is where we ought to focus our attention."

"Do you think we should do that properly? I mean, do we devote most of our attention to the few suppliers in the top right? Or do we dissipate it elsewhere?"

"Gosh. I am not sure. Maybe not."

"You might want to get some analysis done. I would be interested in the result."

"I will do that," agreed Laura. "I will also get to work on how we can use this."

Categorizing Suppliers

In this chapter, we have introduced the TrueSRM framework. This framework is based on differentiated interaction models that are constructed by considering the performance of a supplier and its strategic potential. We have explained that for most companies the existing supplier-performance-management approach is fit for the purpose of enabling the top performers and the poor performers to be differentiated from the majority in the middle. Conversely, most businesses do not have a robust approach in place to determine strategic potential with sufficient rigor. We strongly recommend a top-down approach to this that typically leads to only a very small number of suppliers (often just a couple of handfuls) being classified as high potential.

In the next part of the chapter, we introduced the nine different interaction models that this framework gives rise to. These are discussed as being within three separate clusters. Deploying these models effectively for different suppliers is critical for really bringing TrueSRM to life.

The next three chapters are structured by cluster. For each interaction type, we will explain the key characteristics of suppliers, the types of behaviors that need to be undertaken, and the best ways to work with the suppliers. We will also outline the preferred governance approach and provide a case study example. As we do this, we also continue the story of Heartland as they put their TrueSRM program into effect by deploying the different models.

The "Ordinaries"

Driving Behavior to Get Results

Our tour of the different clusters begins with the "Ordinaries." We start here because this is the area where by far the vast majority of suppliers will be located.

It is also an area that is in danger of being overlooked. Doing so would be a mistake. While you need to beware of overinvesting time and attention on this cluster, don't let the average status of these suppliers fool you. There is strength in numbers here. A keen understanding of what makes these relationships tick, and a simple set of tools for maintaining or incrementally improving their performance, can have sizeable positive results.

Characteristics of Improve Suppliers

The majority of your suppliers are likely to fit here.

Sustain suppliers are interesting and promising from the perspective of relationship potential. Harvest suppliers are not so interesting from the perspective of relationship potential but perform well at what they do. Improve suppliers (Figure 5-1) are interesting in terms of neither. They have very limited promise and there are shortcomings in their performance.

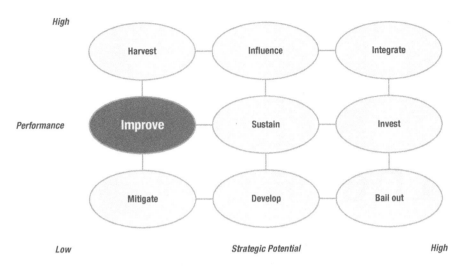

Figure 5-1. Improve suppliers on the strategy/performance axes

Improve suppliers are typically the suppliers that many organizations have in the more basic purchasing areas. They supply commodity-style products and services that are not core to the customer's competitive advantage. Their share of your wallet is likely to be relatively low but may not be in all cases. Your importance to them is likely to vary. Improve suppliers typically range from small and medium-sized enterprises (SMEs), who are highly dependent on a small number of customers, through to large corporations that serve many thousands of different clients.

The common theme is that their performance is broadly acceptable but not stunning. And, as with Sustain suppliers, there may be a history of missing deadlines or occasional quality issues that have left a sour taste in the mouth. The issues have not been so dramatic as to warrant the need to replace the supplier, but nor can the supplier be described as an "unsung hero" in the way that Harvest suppliers can be.

For these reasons, an Improve supplier will not make it into the innermost circle of suppliers from the perspective of the company. Should an Improve supplier fail—especially repeatedly—then you would be very likely to replace it. The Improve relationship can feel quite unstable as a result.

What Kind of Behavior to Drive

Usually, the preferred behavior is for an Improve supplier to address its shortcomings and move toward becoming a Harvest supplier. This is usually preferable to incurring the costs and dislocation of replacement.

The exception to this is if the investment and resource commitment associated with the behavior change is disproportionate to the benefit the customer will receive. In that situation, replacement might become the right option. However, it still needs to be thought about carefully given that identifying alternative superstar suppliers is often challenging and not guaranteed to be successful, and will incur search costs. Companies often spend time fruitlessly looking for the holy grail of the ideal supplier. For Improve suppliers, this is rarely the right option.

Note   It is usually preferable to help an Improve supplier become a Harvest supplier. It is less expensive than "firing" the supplier and finding a new one, whose performance isn't guaranteed to be an improvement.

How to Work with Improve Suppliers

Similarly to Sustain suppliers, the challenge with Improve suppliers is to strike the right balance between investment and return from the relationship. The calculation is one that is more finely poised because you value the relationship potential less and are more likely to replace the supplier. You need to be very clear and straightforward in how you deal with the Improve supplier. Clearly communicate how it needs to perform more effectively. Be candid about its future potential. Otherwise, these suppliers will lack a true understanding of the situation and fail to improve, leading to the more laborious task for you of replacing them.

Governance

The effort dedicated to managing the relationship needs to be kept within clear bounds while still facilitating the sending of very clear signals. Regular review meetings with a candid exchange of dialogue will be sufficient governance to enable this. Typically, we would not expect these to be needed more than biannually.

Case Example

Consider the situation of a supplier of simple low-value parts such as fastenings. This product is not the source of a unique advantage for the customer, but the parts need to be available or else production will be interrupted. However, the supplier has a track record of missing delivery deadlines from several hours up to a day. This is not catastrophic because the manufacturer knows about this behavior and mitigates its own risk by maintaining an inventory of fastenings on hand to give it an adequate safety margin. Additionally, the value of fastenings is low. So, the working-capital implications of a few extra days inventory do not cause major alarm for the finance function. Nevertheless, this behavior is frustrating. It causes extra resources to be deployed to manage inventory, costs money in terms of inventory holding, and leads to queries being raised via enterprise-resource planning software and the operational buyers in the plant each time a deadline is missed.

Despite this major shortcoming, the correct approach is unlikely to be to replace the supplier concerned without making some attempt to correct course. If the supplier does supply fastenings that meet the quality needs to specification, there is no guarantee from a tender process that any new supplier would do this equally as well and no certainty that the delivery issues would be solved. Indeed, more risks may be introduced and there would be a significant cost of replacement. Additionally, it is even possible that there is an element of "six of one and half a dozen of the other" with respect to the problems. There may be misunderstanding over agreed lead times and delivery windows that is contributing to the problems.

The approach that is likely to be most fruitful here is to communicate very clearly to an executive at the supplier's organization that current performance on delivery is unacceptable. At the same time, the messages need to allow for the possibility that you, the customer, may need to help the supplier do this—by, for example, adjusting its behavior and potentially agreeing on different delivery windows or clarifying precisely what its requirements are. The level of help the customer would be prepared to give would probably not have to go too far beyond these measures in order to be cost-effective. There also needs to be a clear message that if performance does not improve then the supplier is at serious risk of being replaced.

Heartland Tackles Procurement

Thomas was about to wrap up the day's work when Laura peeked into his office. "Do you have a couple of minutes?" she asked.

Laura had learned that the easiest way to get Thomas's attention was to walk into his office early in the morning or late in the afternoon. Given that she had been his closest associate in his path to the top at Heartland, Laura still felt that this was the right thing to do rather than formally asking for an appointment.

"Sure, Laura, but I will need to leave in 15 minutes. Both Johanna and David are performing in a play at school tonight. Pretty exciting."

Laura put a graph in front of Thomas. "Take a look at this. I had my staff perform a quick analysis of where we have allocated our procurement resources. As I expected, most of our people are dealing with suppliers on the left-hand side of our SRM framework. With some regional variation, we actually have more than 70 percent of our people dealing with suppliers in Improve. I had expected the overall pattern, but I was surprised by how extreme this picture is. We need to do something."

With his eyes still fixated on the graph, Thomas nodded in agreement. "What do you suggest?"

"Do you remember those initiatives that companies used to run to free people from administrative work and focus them more on strategic topics? I think we need to do something along these lines. Why should we employ hundreds of people dealing with suppliers that don't make any difference while we hardly have anyone working with the ones that really matter?"

Now, Thomas looked up. "I know that tone in your voice," he said with a smile. "What are you up to?"

"I want to take this opportunity to completely reshuffle and upgrade our procurement function," Laura replied. "We will free up a lot of our staff by scaling back the interaction with Improve and other Ordinary suppliers. But just repurposing these people will not do it because most of them lack the required skill set. My proposal is the following: Over the next 12 months, we take out 40 percent of the headcount. With the available budget, I want to hire high-caliber people from consultancies, investment banks, and industry. Also, I want to start recruiting talent at the top MBA schools. According to my scenario, we will end up with an overall much reduced headcount in procurement. Of course, the new people I intend to bring in will be substantially more expensive than our current average, but we will still be below the current budget. They will have the more rounded skill sets that are needed to manage relationships internally and externally and get full value from the more strategic suppliers."

Thomas responded dubiously. "Do you really want to do this at this point in time? You have only been in your CPO role six months."

"Thomas, you and I know that there never is a good 'point in time' to do this. And you have been pretty determined to get things changed in various places. Why make an exception for procurement? I don't expect you to make this type of decision right away, but I wanted to let you know where my head is. Can we put this on the agenda for our next Senior Leadership Team (SLT) meeting?"

It took a lot more than just one meeting of Heartland's senior leadership team for Laura to get the ball rolling. The executives were immediately convinced by the logic of her pitch to restructure the function so as focus far more energy on managing Integrate and other Critical Cluster suppliers, but they remained concerned about the unforeseen consequences of such a deep cut in procurement. Laura was assigned a task force of corporate development and HR people to conduct a detailed analysis of roles, responsibilities, and skill sets. Internal stakeholders were interviewed about procurement's expectations concerning Critical Cluster suppliers. After three months of intensive work, Laura reported back to the SLT with findings that just about confirmed her initial hypothesis.

Seeing the broad intent behind Laura's plans, Thomas finally gave his approval to put the plan in action. Considering the magnitude of the task at hand, Thomas asked John McGrath, his trusted advisor, to coach Laura through the challenges of reshuffling an organization of more than 1,500 people scattered across the globe. Nine months into the program, Laura proudly reported the following status to the SLT:

- A reduction of activities devoted to managing Improve suppliers had been completed—the number of incidents or complaints: zero.

- The headcount had been freed up to manage Integrate and other Critical Cluster suppliers more effectively: out of 571 employees, 221 had been transferred to roles in other functions outside of procurement, 209 had accepted a voluntary separation package, and 141 had been transferred to other roles within procurement.

- Thirty-seven senior hires were in place to fill new strategic roles for Influence, Integrate, and Invest suppliers.

- There had been 28 recruits from top-ranking business schools.

Characteristics of Sustain Suppliers

Together with Improve, Harvest, and to a certain extent Mitigate, Sustain forms the more densely populated area of the SRM framework. For a company with 1,000 suppliers, we would expect to find dozens of Sustain suppliers.

Generally speaking, suppliers in Sustain (Figure 5-2) are interesting and promising. Their strategic potential is higher than that of the vast majority of suppliers working with the company. The products and services these suppliers provide are essential for the company's position in the market and there might even be the potential to do more with them. This places them above the majority of the company's suppliers. It also distinguishes them from Improve suppliers—it is much more challenging to replace them. That means that you need to invest more in the relationship but without overdoing things.

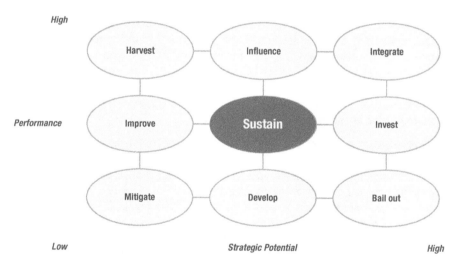

Figure 5-2. Sustain suppliers on the strategy/performance axes

Despite this above-average strategic potential though, this supplier still has not made it into the innermost circle of suppliers from the perspective of the company. Unlike with Critical Cluster suppliers, you are not leveraging major competitive advantage from the relationship. However, the positioning of the supplier within the category of Strategic Potential suggests that you could. The reason you are not doing so is that performance is just average. You may even have tried to give the supplier opportunities to do more and provide more value to your business. But the supplier has not been able to perform when given those opportunities. In hindsight, those attempts were certainly not disasters but they left a bit of a sour taste behind. The supplier may have slipped deadlines, there may have been some quality issues that were contained, or the resulting service or product may not have fully met customer expectations. You are now wary of offering further opportunities to the supplier along the same lines.

Based on this average performance, the supplier is now used for average tasks. It would be awarded with contracts for mainstream products and services that are not as exciting as the really-hot-and-new stuff the company stands for. That position may even give the supplier a fairly large chunk of the available business. So, superficially things will look good from a supplier perspective, and only a closer look at profit margins would reveal the untapped opportunities.

What Kind of Behavior to Drive

The desired behavior to use with the Sustain supplier needs to be determined by the overall context. Provided that there are alternative suppliers that perform at a higher level and are positioned in Influence, there might not be the need to change a lot of things. In that case, the supplier would be encouraged to work on its performance with the company's minimal involvement. After all, there are no major fixes needed and the company has learned to live with the few shortcomings the supplier has. Both parties may be content with this status quo.

However, that may not be the case. You may feel that you really need more active innovation in the product areas that the supplier provides. This is more likely to occur if you have no Influence supplier in these areas. In this case, you would want to give the supplier far-more active encouragement to increase performance to world-class levels. If there already is an Influence supplier in these product areas, then you would not expend this effort. It would not be worth your while. You might even decide to encourage the Influence supplier to expand its scope. That would be a potential threat for the Sustain supplier.

How to Work with Sustain Suppliers

The challenge of working with Sustain suppliers is to strike the right balance between investment and return. When these suppliers recognize what you value about working with them, they will be less likely to become complacent and allow their performance to slip or to present less desirable commercial terms to you. Always treat the Sustain supplier fairly while not tying up disproportionate resources. The relationship is likely to be relatively arm's-length, with the supplier needing to compete for additional business. However, take care in this respect. Market and performance changes can cause shifts in the relationship. Remaining sufficiently close to the supplier will help you understand this dynamic and act accordingly.

Note   Achieving the right balance between investment in a Sustain supplier and the return on that investment is a moving target. As the market and the supplier's performance change, you will need to adjust the dial frequently to get the best results. That requires staying close to the supplier to make the right moves.

Governance

Since there are probably dozens of suppliers in Sustain for an average company, the effort dedicated to managing the relationship for each needs to be kept at bay. For the majority of suppliers, the key platform for alignment will be quarterly reviews. In these reviews, the company will give the supplier feedback on its performance against a set of predetermined criteria. The supplier will then provide an update of key initiatives and progress against plan.

For Sustain suppliers that lack competitors in the Influence box, quarterly reviews still might be the right forum, but there should be a different emphasis in the message that is delivered to them. The company should outline very clear and specific expectations regarding what it takes to reach world-class performance.

Here, it is important to consider what improvements the company can realistically trigger in a Sustain supplier. Most likely, the Sustain supplier will provide a product or a service that is deemed essential for a certain industry. Therefore, this supplier will have working relationships with many customers in that industry and your company will not have an overwhelming importance for it. Considering this, the company will not be able to provide more than a nudge to move in the direction of world-class performance. The main initiative and momentum needs to be created by the supplier on its own.

Case Example

Anyone driving through Riverside County up to Palm Springs, California, cannot help but be impressed by the large array of turbines in the San Gorgonio Pass Wind Farm. This gateway into the Coachella Valley is one of the windiest regions in Southern California. This wind farm contains more than 4,000 separate turbines and, with a capacity of 360 megawatts, provides enough electricity to power Palm Springs and the entire Coachella Valley.

San Gorgonio is by far not the largest wind farm in the world. California alone has two wind farms that are larger. The world record for onshore wind farms is currently held by the Gansu Wind Farm in China, with a capacity of 5,000 MW. The biggest offshore wind farm is the London Array with 630 MW. For comparison, the largest nuclear reactor in the world is currently being built in Olkiluoto, Finland. Once fully operational, its capacity will be 1,600 MW.

With many large wind farms under construction, let's take a look at the relationship between the typical developer of a wind farm and the typical turbine maker. All starts with the developer identifying a suitable piece of land. The developer will begin by collecting detailed wind patterns by specific location, height, and day. The most desired outcome of these analyses is steady wind throughout the year, not varying over day and night.

Based on the confirmed wind patterns, engineering consulting firms will then configure the wind park. By specific location, they will plan the most optimal turbine. Some locations within the wind park will be more suitable for tall and big turbines; others will be more suitable for smaller turbines on shorter towers.

On average, a wind turbine extracts 44 percent of the kinetic energy of the wind flowing through the turbine. The science is well understood and there is not much room for differentiation between the makers of turbines. With that, the typical turbine supplier would have average strategic potential and therefore fall into the middle column of the SRM framework.

In terms of performance, the overwhelming majority of turbine suppliers will fall into the average category. Given the volatile nature of the wind industry, it is challenging for suppliers to perform flawlessly. Wind farm projects are notoriously late. Normally, it takes the developer more time than expected to get all the required approvals and financing put in place. The turbine supplier can only wait and hope for the best. Usually, the order confirmation finally comes in when internal capacities are already booked for other contracts. This up and down makes it difficult to achieve process stability. In addition, local legislation often requires substantial modifications to the structural, electrical, and hydraulic components of the turbine.

The usual headaches for wind farm developers when dealing with turbine suppliers are delivery delays, cost creeps, and quality problems. None of these usually get too serious and eventually every wind farm gets up and running.

The relationship between the developer and the turbine supplier usually does not become very close. From the developer's point of view, identifying the right piece of land, matching turbine types with wind patterns, getting the approvals, and securing the financing are the core activities, and the turbine supplier comes in after all of those steps are taken care of. So when the turbine supplier is ramping up, the developer is already ramping down. Of course, operational personnel from the developer will monitor the supplier to ensure that it is delivering to specification.

In summary, the relationship between the wind farm developer and the turbine supplier fits into the Sustain supplier interaction model squarely. The supplier is essential to the developer, but at least from today's technological point of view, there is no way to fundamentally differentiate and to create a winning ecosystem. With the volatile environment in the business, chances are that the developer will hardly ever be enthusiastic about the performance of the supplier but will regard it as necessary.

Heartland Begins to Deploy TrueSRM

As the restructuring of procurement was coming toward a close, Laura started to turn her attention more to how the TrueSRM framework would be deployed. As part of the restructuring, Laura had created a very small central function in procurement that had responsibility for tools and processes. This was now led by Blair Worden, reporting directly to Laura in her role as procurement COO. Blair had joined procurement from Heartland's finance function, where he had previously been the commercial finance head for the European business. He was charged with implementing the framework. Given the importance of TrueSRM to the business, however, Laura maintained a very strong interest in the detail. Blair brought a perspective beyond procurement. Although he was a career finance professional, he had also held previous roles in marketing and IT, and he was on Heartland's fast-track development path.

Blair inherited the initial rough supplier segmentation that had been carried out to support the original activity analysis that had prompted the decision to restructure. Laura and Blair decided to take a strong, top-down approach to reviewing the segmentation rather than the very bottom-up, category-by-category approach that often leads to each category vying to name suppliers in the Critical Cluster. While this may make sense for the individual category, it rarely works from a corporate perspective and can lead to the perverse result of facilities suppliers, for example, being classified as Integrate. Laura and Blair decided to work through each interaction model one by one, both to validate the suppliers that were classified in it and to drive the right interventions that would need to be executed by the category leaders responsible for it.

They chose to start in the Ordinaries cluster. Laura felt that Thomas did not need to be involved in any significant way here, although other functional leaders would clearly be very much part of the implementation.

After the Improve suppliers, Sustain was the most populous model. Laura and Blair convened in Laura's office to discuss what to do. Addressing the groups was actually surprisingly tricky.

Laura laid out her perspective: "We really don't want to put too much effort into these guys," she said, referring to the Sustain suppliers. "But they do have more value to us than the Improve suppliers. I mean some of our major IT vendors sit here."

"I agree," said Blair. "I am sure some of them could contribute far more to our business than they do currently. We need to encourage and support them to do this but not at the expense of disproportionate effort our side."

"We need to nudge them," added Laura.

"I think that mandating some very clear scorecards that show our view of them, with a clear message, would work here," Blair suggested.

"We need to keep it simple, though," said Laura. "I do not want to create a paper chase with people pursuing metrics, reconciling numbers, and debating statistics. That would defeat what we are trying to achieve."

Blair thought for a moment or two. He then added: "Maybe we just make it very transparent to them how we see their position. We communicate that there are issues that have prevented us from awarding them more business and that they need to up their game if they are to continue with us."

"Yes, a simple score card that records our view of them is probably enough. We can combine that with a quarterly review session that the suppliers lead and a business representative attends. The review session will also give the opportunity for a two-way dialogue, and for the supplier to explain its perspective."

"OK." said Blair. "I will start to contact the category leaders to make that happen. We might also want to think about providing some training so as to help the category leaders treat the reviews as genuine two-way dialogues rather than pure information-giving sessions."

"Good idea. Let's capture that," agreed Laura. "I am sure we will also have additional training needs as we go through the other models. Harvest is next . . . ."

Characteristics of Harvest Suppliers

Harvest suppliers are typically thinner on the ground than the other Ordinaries. For a company with 1,000 suppliers, we would not expect to find more than a couple of dozen of them in this interaction model.

Suppliers in Harvest (Figure 5-3) can be seen as "unsung heroes." Their performance is excellent but the actual potential relationship value is low. They supply goods or services that the company needs to have but that are not highly critical to its commercial success. The most basic cross-industry example of a Harvest supplier might be the distributor of stationery to the company's offices; it always happens on time, the cost performance is fine, and if it stopped everyone would notice. But, there is not some great yearning need for the customer to tap greater value from the relationship through innovation. Indeed, if the supplier did innovate significantly, we may not even notice or might struggle to see the value.

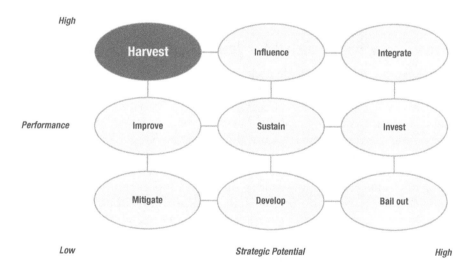

Figure 5-3. Harvest suppliers on the strategy/performance axes

So, despite its strong performance, this supplier has not made it into the innermost circle of suppliers from the perspective of the company. Nor can it ever hope to. Mature and sensible Harvest suppliers realize that this is the reality and manage accordingly. They are used to their status as unsung heroes and focus on performance as the only way to retain and win additional contracts. Their share of wallet with any individual customer can vary significantly. The common feature is that Harvest suppliers operate in category areas that are usually not strategic for the business, such as telecommunications, facilities management, and utilities. These are all areas that for most businesses are essential services that are noticed if they fail but for which there is no real need to drive exclusive innovation. Accordingly, the Harvest suppliers focus on serving a very large number of customers to build scale and to hedge their bets in case any particular customer chooses to stop working with them. They will value their relationship with you but will typically not overinvest in it.

What Kind of Behavior to Drive

The desired behavior of the Harvest suppliers needs to be determined in the overall context. Assuming you have correctly determined that the potential relationship value is low, then the desired behavior is to "carry on as is." There is no need to change anything nor to rock the boat.

This means that you need the Harvest supplier to maintain its current strong performance and not to falter. You need it to value the relationship with you sufficiently enough that it is incentivized to continue to perform.

How to Work with Harvest Suppliers

Whereas the trick to working with Sustain suppliers is to invest enough effort in the relationship to maintain the performance level while not inadvertently sending a signal that you want to "partner," most Harvest suppliers are sufficiently mature that they will continue to perform with very limited encouragement from the customer. They are used to doing this for a large number of other customers too and will happily do the same for you if you let them. Harvest suppliers are also used to having to justify their continued presence through competitive tender; the possible threat of which (if not overdone) can provide a continued goad to best-in-class performance on quality, service, and economic dimensions.

Things tend to go wrong when individual buyers in companies overfocus on the relationship and miscommunicate the true position. This sometimes happens when customers apply supplier segmentation at a category level and do not force an organization-wide calibration. We have seen situations where well-performing suppliers of mundane items get wrongly labeled as partners. This is often as a result of overenthusiastic category managers in nonstrategic categories wanting to apply partnership approaches inappropriately. Such behavior inevitably leads eventually to frustration and misalignment on both sides. In particular, the Harvest supplier may misinterpret such signals as an indication that it can charge a premium price beyond that which is justified by its strong performance and competitive advantage in its category. Ultimately, this would be self-defeating.

Harvest suppliers illustrate in the most extreme case the broad injunction associated with the Ordinaries cluster, "Leave well enough alone."

Tip Value your Harvest suppliers and praise them when appropriate as the unsung heroes they are. But do not encourage them to think of themselves as partners. In most cases, the products they offer are not important, strategic inputs to your key initiatives.

Governance

Typically, biannual reviews will be sufficient platforms for governance. In these reviews, the company will give the supplier feedback on its performance against a set of predetermined criteria. It will also give encouragement that continued strong performance will be rewarded and that reduced performance can be dealt with through competition.

We would not expect the governance discussions to go beyond these points. There is neither a significant need for you to discuss initiatives that will build the relationship nor to involve senior leadership other than specific functional experts such as the head of facilities. Depending on its actual scale of business with you, the Harvest supplier may involve senior executives from its side, but you need not be tempted to match this in most normal situations.

The real challenge with managing the governance meetings is to stay focused on the themes that matter for this interaction model. Overenthusiasm needs to be reined in on both sides. This will avoid frustration and inappropriate behavior. Typically, candor that the supplier is in the Harvest state will be helpful as part of these forums. An intelligent Harvest supplier will not push back on this but will welcome the clarity that you are providing.

Case Example

Let's consider a mundane example of a service that every business requires: facilities management. This is an essential service that involves ensuring facilities are cleaned, guarded, and maintained properly. It also often includes energy management. Usually, this is something that senior executives do not want to spend time thinking about. A number of different organizations offer "service"-based solutions. Typically, these suppliers each have a large number of customers whose share of wallet will vary based on the characteristics of the business. The category is also highly competitive and the service level is critical. Poor performance can lead to contract cancellation—although usually customers seek to avoid this if they can, given the costs of dislocation that would be incurred.

If one looks at the sales messages of the suppliers concerned, the whole pitch is associated with outsourcing a headache so that you as a customer do not have to worry about it. These suppliers understand their core business model. They give messages associated with "quiet efficiency," "supporting businesses," and "one-stop shopping"—focusing on how to make life easy for their customers.

Innovation from these suppliers is focused on taking these service-related concepts still further to enable you as a customer to worry even less about the category in the future. They drive the innovation themselves for all of their customers and it does not need your help or input to create, although you may need to take some action in order to tap into it. An example of this would be a top-performing facilities supplier that brings to you as a customer a smart metering solution that enables energy consumption to be controlled. This would ideally be combined with bidirectional control and data analytics to ensure that energy-usage policies can be optimized, set, and consistently implemented across your estate. Such solutions can lead to double-digit percentage savings in energy consumption. Valuable as these savings are, they do not lead to a game-changing improvement in the competitiveness of the end product for the vast majority of companies. Furthermore, the supplier has no incentive in any event to offer an individual customer some form of exclusivity or unique advantage even if you do value its service. In its market, it needs to serve everyone equally well and must "play the field" in order to create scale and profit.

The supplier doing this work will be high performing but is still in the Harvest category in terms of relationship potential; it performs strongly in its function and its failure would be rapidly noticed, but there is no real opportunity for the customer to broaden the relationship as a way to obtain significant competitive advantage in the marketplace.

Heartland Scales Back Overinvestment of Time

Laura and Blair were now considering the Harvest suppliers. One of the suppliers included on the top-down segmentation was Facilities R Us, the office-facilities supplier that organized cleaning and washroom services for Heartland. Laura fixed her gaze on the supplier: "It makes sense that we classified it as Harvest," she said. "I know that it performs very well and we never seem to have any issues."

"The category team talks about it as a 'strategic partner' though," commented Blair. "The team and the corporate-services function see Facilities R Us as contributing huge amounts of value-added input. I know that they have lots of meetings with the supplier. There was even an Innovation Day last year."

"Yes," said Laura. "This is one of the cases where there is overinvestment in and too much effort being spent on this supplier. It is supplying something pretty basic very well, but it does not contribute to how we grow the top line."

"Do you think it is our fault, or theirs, that there is all this effort?" Blair asked her.

"Probably six of one and a half dozen of the other. I always believe that you get the supplier behavior that you deserve. I suspect that Facilities R Us is responding to the steering we have given it as a customer. We are a large account for them. The company's sales manager will no doubt be very happy to attend any meeting we want to set up and quite frankly indulge our whims. The point is that we need to be more focused and disciplined as a business here. Facilities R Us delivers well but we create process around it that is excessive and probably distracting more than anything else. "

"Yes," agreed Blair. "I am sure we will find the same thing with other Harvest suppliers."

"We need to scale back the meetings here, recognize the mundaneness of what the supplier is doing, and allow it to do its job. I also suspect the company is incurring excess cost to support this account, and its chances of winning real incremental business are low. I mean it is a facilities business, and it has our core contract. There is not really anything else to give them."

"I will work with the category team to get this in shape," Blair resolved. "We need to communicate to the supplier how we really see the company. Then they can get on with the job we really want done."

Blair then thought for a second and added: "Say, if the company can cut down on the effort it has to devote to managing us, then perhaps we ought to be asking for better commercial terms to reflect that, too?"

Laura laughed. "Maybe we should," she said, "but not straightaway, I think!"

Rethink Relations with Ordinaries

In this chapter, we have described the three interaction models that characterize the Ordinaries. As we have seen, these will constitute the vast majority of suppliers to your business. The trick for managing these suppliers is to balance the level of investment you put into the relationship with the potential returns.

We started with the Ordinaries precisely because we do not want to ignore them. It is all too easy to do that when one turns to the other clusters that distinguish themselves more readily. This distinction is a positive one for the Critical Cluster because of the high potential value you can achieve from working with them. It is negative in the case of the Problematics, where serious fixes are needed.

We will turn our attention in Chapter 6 to the challenging Problematic Suppliers. We will then address the grassy uplands of the Critical Cluster in Chapter 7.

"Problem Children"

Addressing Problematic Supplier Relationships

From a psychological point of view, children are often called problem children if they are not able to manage everyday challenges and problems, or if they are not performing as expected in their environment.

It is already a given in science that problem children are not always suffering from a disease; on the contrary, these children often tend to be highly intelligent. It is important to understand the real root causes. They are not able to show their potential because they are not challenged and valued enough. Their capabilities need to be fostered and promoted. They need support and should be sponsored to perform successfully.

The other case that occurs is that these problem children are just too slow to keep up with their peer group. Sometimes this is just because of laziness.

It is really difficult for parents to distinguish which group the child belongs in—and determining that is exactly the art in the diagnosis. The same principles are true for the bottom group in the supplier interaction matrix, Mitigate, Develop, and Bail Out.

Suppliers in each of these models have important characteristics in common:

1. Their current performance is very low.

2. They need significant care and risk management.

The analogy to the children just mentioned holds here as well: some are lazy, some are having real problems, and some are super smart but choosing not to show their capabilities. Yet you must be able to assess the strategic value that the supplier brings. This is the key challenge. Is the supplier the highly intelligent child, with great innovations or new technologies used on behalf of their client companies but just overstrained in daily business? In this case, considering this supplier a Bail Out would make sense to utilize the strategic potential as competitive advantage. If the performance of a well-known supplier with very limited strategic potential is sluggish, then tagging that supplier a Mitigate is the answer. The supplier needs to understand that either it improves and rises to the occasion or it is out. If we find that a supplier has performance somewhere in between low and high strategic potential, then Develop could be the best interaction model to place it in. This would mean that the supplier will be nurtured so as to perform more effectively.

The competitive advantage of successful companies—just as with successful psychologists—is that they identify very fast which type of problem child they have in front of them and they make immediate, rigorous decisions on the way forward.

Characteristics of Mitigate Suppliers

Mitigate is an area of the SRM framework where we normally find around 5 percent of all suppliers. For a company with 1,000 suppliers, we would accordingly expect to find dozens of suppliers in this interaction model.

In general, suppliers in Mitigate (Figure 6-1) have low strategic potential. The products and services they provide represent no clear differentiating factor for the company's position in the market. While the majority of suppliers share this characteristic, those in Mitigate need much closer attention than those in Improve or Harvest.

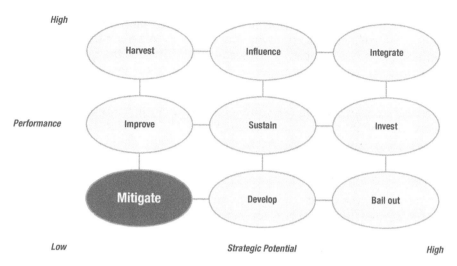

Figure 6-1. Mitigate suppliers

The lack of strategic potential is not the most critical aspect that requires application of the "up or out" rule. The real challenge is that Mitigate suppliers have severe performance issues. Delivery, cost, and/or quality show permanent shortcomings over time. This is why the downside potential with such suppliers is tremendous. We find this position in all sorts of suppliers. Quite often, they are large suppliers with commoditized products and may even be long-lasting relationships. The overall attention that the supplier gives you decreases, however, as they pursue and acquire emerging new customers. Alternatively, they just become complacent.

Based on the low strategic value and poor performance, there is an immediate need for action. The supplier needs to understand it has to improve performance—to move "up"—or it will be replaced—moved "out." This is why a solid contingency plan for replacement is an integrated element of this interaction model.

Needless to say, a large portion of risk management is closely linked with this area of SRM. This is done to mitigate both the consequences of poor performance and the dislocation issues associated with replacement.

What Kind of Behavior to Drive

While most of the other interaction models have one clear desired behavior, there are a couple of options in this case. Specifically, we need to distinguish between the up behavior and the out behavior for the supplier. The supplier commonly needs to understand the necessity for changing its behavior and the consequences related to it. Of course, the most desired behavior for Mitigate is a supplier that improves and delivers a solid performance and improves shortcomings in a very short period of time without the company's involvement. But what if the supplier either fails or is not willing to improve, and so needs to be replaced?

In that case, the desired behavior is for the supplier to remain professional, transparent, and open in the replacement and in the transition period. At least some of the performance issues need to be stabilized, requiring some short-term fixes. Some significant oversight by the company is necessary in the replacement phase—on the one hand to fix the issues for the next supplier and on the other hand to ensure a smooth transition.

Paradoxically, the quality of such a relationship—even though it is ending—is one of the most important ones in SRM because you need to maintain a level of openness and clarity while you are still working together.

Note When you have decided to switch to a different supplier, you and the incumbent both need to operate with clarity and good intentions. When a supplier knows it is being edged out, that's not the easiest situation to handle for either party.

How to Work with Mitigate Suppliers

Suppliers in Mitigate are given a final chance to improve, but there will be very limited guidance because they are simply not worth the effort. The dissatisfaction with the supplier needs to be communicated and fact based. The supplier needs to clearly understand how serious the situation is. Then, you give it an opportunity to improve. If they do not take it, you need to move them out.

While the up portion of this interaction model is very much about suppliers improving performance on their own, the challenge is the out portion. The main ingredient to being successful in this interaction model is transparency. You especially need to understand interdependencies across different lines of business/business units or within different categories. The impact of bringing in a potential replacement needs to be intelligently evaluated. Be aware that, for example, some of the supporting processes or services of the supplier are not always obvious. A potential exit needs to be aligned and supported by stakeholders. Guidance for this alignment will most probably be scenarios, business cases, and contingency plans based on an anticipated supplier reaction.

For example, you need to be prepared for the supplier to become even less focused on your needs in this period. The team that has currently been serving your needs within the organization may gravitate to different customers, for example. Performance may degrade still further. You need to be prepared for these eventualities and be able to ramp up a replacement option more quickly than originally expected.

Once the supplier receives word of the transition, your desire is that this will fulfill all remaining business obligations and articulate steps for handing off the business to a new supplier rather than create problems. Typically, you would agree on a joint transition plan that will be executed by the supplier being replaced in cooperation with the new supplier. Usually, suppliers manage exits professionally. It is bad for their reputation to cause intentional problems. Issues tend to be most likely when the supplier being replaced is relatively small and is either captive to you or has a small number of customers in total. In this situation, the supplier's wider reputation is less important for it and it has more to lose by being replaced. The risk of a tricky exit is consequently higher.

Once the transition plan is in place and being executed, the most important—but also the most difficult—success factor in the transition is to remain professional. Displays of emotions on both the supplier and the buyer side are inappropriate. Be sure to get a view on the supplier's inner state; the supplier needs to be as transparent as a pane of glass.

Last but not least, it is key not to leave a battlefield behind. Keep the relationship alive with a view for future business. Usually, the supplier will be keen to do this, too.

Governance

As each company has dozens of suppliers in Mitigate, we have to distinguish between the effort related to Mitigate in the up and the out sections. As we have already discussed, the positioning of a supplier in Mitigate can become really critical for the company and fast actions need to be readied. In most cases, there is no time to wait for a quarterly or annual review meeting. You need to get into contact with the supplier once the shortcomings are realized. The purpose will be to ask the supplier to provide a mitigation plan against which its performance improvement will be measured.

In those cases where the supplier is not able to realize an up, the transition comes into place. In the transition, it is key to ask the supplier to update you on every aspect of the phasing out. Depending on the scope and the expected time of replacement, it makes sense to have regular meetings with the supplier just as you would with a state-of-the-art project management team. This encompasses aspects such as achievements to date, identified obstacles, problems, and mitigation planning. Most meetings of this type only take place between the existing supplier and the client, but it turns out to be much more effective if the new supplier is involved, too. Supplier facilities, inventory levels, order volumes, or quality fulfillments need to be monitored closely as part of integrated risk management during the implementation. If severe problems occur during the transition, a task force has to be put in place at the supplier to secure supply.

Case Example

When you had your last yogurt, did you think about the complexity of the box and the lid? Probably not. Nevertheless, a yogurt lid is something quite interesting and manufacturing one could cause a lot of trouble with the supplier. Some background on the lid: the structure is mainly based on aluminum, printing ink, lacquers, and a layer of varnish.

Varnish is a mostly glossy or semiglossy, transparent finish that is used to protect and to finish. It normally has no color pigments in it. Ingredients of varnishes are kept highly confidential. In general, their production is not a rocket science and the type of varnish used is in most cases not a differentiating factor. End customers do not even know that there are different varieties. What's more, the yogurt producers do not care about the varnish producer. The varnish is supplied to a flexible packaging manufacturer that then supplies the yogurt producer. So, is the varnish quite a simple product? Is it then easy to change varnish suppliers? Not risky at all?

Generally speaking, for varnishes this is true, but it is much more complicated if you look further into this specific case. In yogurts, the varnish has contact with food, and as some people tend to have the habit to lick the yogurt from the lid, they are also in direct contact with the varnish, meaning that the varnish needs to have FDA (US Food and Drug Administration) approval. The FDA's approvals of the products it regulates are as varied as the products themselves. These differences are dictated by the laws the FDA enforces and the relative risks that the products pose to consumers. Beside FDA approval, another thing to know is that varnishes show different reactions over time. Even with sophisticated laboratory methods, it is not possible to simulate. Long-term tests must be undertaken.

Given these facts, the suppliers of varnish to flexible packaging producers tend to consider themselves as being in a very secure position. This is not because of the uniqueness of the product itself but because approval processes for new products limit a buyer's choices. The strategic value of the supplier is therefore rather limited, but the downside potential if the supplier causes trouble is quite high.

With this background in mind, one varnish supplier started a dangerous journey. It increased prices step-by-step—in some negotiation rounds even double digit. But the service quality of the supplier was decreasing and delivery issues started. The customer was obliged to hold significant inventory levels of varnish in order to overcome bottlenecks. Up to this point it had done so, since it was clear that no varnish means no production. When the supplier threatened to stop supply, the customer realized that it was time to deliver an up or out message. Even the supplier's biggest supporters in production supported this approach.

The supplier was invited to a meeting with the management team and its shortcomings were made transparent. The potential consequences, like switching away from varnish for new products or even a complete shift to another provider for all products, were not taken seriously by the supplier.

This laissez-faire attitude was not a sensible philosophy. After two months with no improvement, the supplier was informed that it was being replaced. Of course, the customer did not only wait but used the time wisely to prepare the phaseout. The transparency that was created made clear that not only the yogurt lids were affected by a potential shift but also some other products ordered from the same supplier that had the varnish in their specifications. In total, approximately 3,000 recipes the customer produced for different clients were affected by the replacement.

A transition plan was created for all products. In addition, suppliers that were identified to be replacements were partly involved. The supplier was a bit surprised and shocked that the replacement scenario came into place and was taken seriously by the customer. During the replacement meeting, as a reaction the management of the supplier showed willingness to commit to improve performance, but as previous promises did not show the desired effect, the customer did not change its decision. In the end, the management of the supplier promised to support the transition process professionally. It kept that promise.

The supplier contributed to and formally signed the detailed transition plan and agreed to regular reviews. The process was only marred by an attempt on the part of the supplier's sales manager to raise prices. This was refused after escalation on the customer side. After 18 months, the transition was complete. The company saved one-third of its original spending on varnish and got access to an innovative and highly motivated supplier, which did not just copy the former varnish but improved the specifications to achieve better workability and longer duration. This made the engineering department happy, because while it supported the process, it was a bit skeptical as to whether the company was making the right move.

In summary, the relationship between the customer and the varnish supplier was clearly in the Mitigate supplier interaction model. The supplier was not performing in terms of price and delivery performance.

After being prewarned several times, the supplier was replaced and a detailed transition plan was executed. Because of how professionally the transition was executed, there was surprisingly little bad blood on either side. In fact, the varnish supplier undertook major internal soul-searching as a result of this experience. It has made a conscious effort to up its game elsewhere. In fact, it is even tendering again to win work with the customer that replaced it.

TrueSRM Comes to Marketing

As part of implementing TrueSRM at Heartland, Procurement initiated reviews with each key part of the business to review the supplier positioning and agree on the actions. Laura attended several of the sessions personally. The marketing meeting was particularly fascinating. Scarlet, in her role as chief marketing officer, attended along with Jane Cavendish from Laura's team, who was responsible for marketing procurement. A number of members of Scarlet's team also attended the session; in fact, it ended up as quite a crowd, which was not unusual for marketing meetings.

Laura had taken the precaution of having a premeeting with Scarlet to discuss the ideas that Procurement was about to put on the table. Scarlet was receptive but she wanted her team to be taken on the journey rather than for her to dictate an outcome to them. The big elephant in the room was that despite its commitment to strategic sourcing, Heartland had not run a full creative agency pitch for some years. This was an area that Thomas had chosen not to tackle as CPO; there had been bigger issues to deal with.

But there was an increasing sense that Heartland was not getting what it needed from the agency relationship and that a change might be needed. This had nothing to do with cost but all to do with the level of creative input that the agency was giving. Quite frankly, Heartland's advertising lacked the freshness of Calbury's, which had won plaudits for making consumers feel good in very simple ways—like the famous example of a gorilla playing the drums to the strains of the '60s Matt Monro hit "Walk Away." Almost unbelievably, this had accounted for a big sales increase. Delta Creative, Heartland's advertising agency, was nowhere near providing this level of creativity. The whole advertising package was very stale. However, not all of Scarlet's team shared this view, even though Scarlet was sympathetic with the view that a change was in order.

The first minor hiccup to be conveyed in the marketing meeting was that the marketing people were surprised that no suppliers were shown as belonging to the Critical Cluster in the top right-hand quadrant of Laura's Three Clusters model, which she presented to the team projected on a screen showing the interaction models and their supplier plots. Jane explained that the categorization was from a corporate perspective rather than a pure functional one. In this light, it had been hard to think of any existing marketing supplier as strongly supporting Heartland's competitive advantage. It was felt that even Delta Creative really only carried out a workman-like role rather than one that strongly differentiated Heartland. The company was accordingly positioned as Sustain. Even Scarlet's marketing team accepted this view after some discussion, during which Laura had to intervene a couple of times in support of Jane.

After a brief coffee break, Laura decided to go on the offensive: "Shouldn't the creative agency be doing more than a workman-like job?" she exclaimed. "I wonder if something needs to be done about it. We have positioned the company as Sustain, but I wonder whether we should really be more aggressive. Its performance does not seem very good at all from what I am hearing. Also, it is not clear that it is attracting the right creative talent, which would mean it could turn things around. Its strategic potential feels limited to me, too."

Laura boldly walked up to the screen showing the interaction models and their supplier plots. She pointed to the bottom left-hand corner and ventured: "Why don't we just face reality? Delta Creative is a Mitigate supplier, which means we really need to replace it. That is the logic of what we're talking about."

For a few moments, there was silence in the room, as everyone took a sharp intake of breath to contemplate what Laura had said. Then, Dean Everley, Scarlet's head of marketing, spoke in his thick Tennessee accent: "Laura," he drawled, "I think you might have a point. Delta Creative is getting a bit long in the tooth. Its creative pipeline is poor and it sees us as a cash cow. Maybe we should replace it and get another agency with newer ideas, a company that is hungry to serve Heartland. I'm not sure we want drumming gorillas, but we sure don't want the nonsense we are currently producing. What do y'all think?"

The dam had well and truly burst. Dean had voiced what others were thinking but could not bring themselves to articulate. The relationship with Delta had gone on so long that no one relished the idea of replacing them and losing some genuine friendships.

There was general agreement though that Delta Creative did need to be replaced. Scarlet had been prepared to force the issue herself if necessary but was happy that the team got there without her pushing them.

The public announcement that would follow saying that Heartland was reconsidering its creative agency relationships was big news in the marketing press, given the size of the account and the longevity of the relationship with Delta Creative. Out of fairness, Delta was given the opportunity to participate in the pitch. But its underperformance counted against the company and they lost the contract. Heartland put in place a transition plan and, to be fair, Delta played its role in the transition professionally. The separation was as amicable as it could be under the circumstances. However, it was no longer a supplier to Heartland.

Delta learned from the experience and later won business with two other smaller and less complex accounts; it vowed not to take them for granted the way it had with Heartland.

Characteristics of Develop Suppliers

Develop suppliers are typically thinner on the ground compared to the rest of the Problematic Suppliers. For a company with 1,000 suppliers, we would not expect to find more than a handful of suppliers in this interaction model. You would not wish to see too many suppliers in this model because that would be indicative of an overall poorly performing supply base.

Generally speaking, suppliers in Develop (Figure 6-2) could become interesting and promising because their strategic potential is slightly higher than that of the vast majority of suppliers working with the company. The products and services these suppliers provide could become important for the company's position in the market. The potential needs to be tapped by identifying opportunities across the value chain of both the supplier and the company. One thing is clear: the supplier is currently not ready for prime time but it has the potential to become a star supplier in the future.

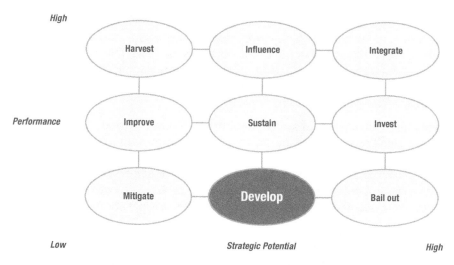

Figure 6-2. Develop suppliers

Suppliers in Develop can also be found in those who have severe operational problems and show performance that is in the back quartile of all suppliers. Yet there is something about them—a spark, an enthusiasm—that separates them from Mitigates. Their poor performance needs to be addressed. It is not a disaster if such a supplier fails but just a lost opportunity.

Recurring performance issues are the reason why there is no competitive advantage and a lack of operational benefits at the moment for the Develop supplier. These issues can be fixed in a way that the company benefits from a supplier. There are numerous examples of Develop suppliers that became key resources in well-managed relationships.

Consider, for example, the many manufacturers that nurture low-cost country suppliers by providing technology or engineering assistance to get them up to speed as component suppliers. Imagine that the supplier fixes its operational problems, which brings great benefit and competitive advantage to these manufacturers—mostly in terms of cost, but also in terms of technology improvements.

What Kind of Behavior to Drive

The desired behavior of the Develop supplier needs to be discussed in the context of future business opportunities. The supplier needs to perceive a unique chance to grow significantly and needs to be willing to follow a given development plan. It is required that the supplier is open to working with the company's people across its organization.

A triangle of trust, confidence, and commitment needs to be in place. The supplier needs trust in the growth opportunity and in the company itself, and believe that the support will be to its benefit. The project leadership in the Develop interaction model from the supplier's side has to be confident that the operational improvements are achievable because the supplier has to drive the improvement.

This leads us to the idea of commitment. Speaking about Develop, with some significant benefit for both sides, it is not something that should be managed as just another initiative by a key account manager. Given the major strategic impact, the management needs to be committed to drive this improvement. The supplier needs to allocate core resources for improving engineering, manufacturing, quality, or operational capabilities.

The supplier should be encouraged to work on its performance with quite a bit of involvement by the company. The recommendations of these resources need to be implemented.

How to Work with Develop Suppliers

The key challenge of working with Develop suppliers is to identify the right organizations, those able to accept the challenge of becoming an important supplier. Because these suppliers receive significant support, there needs to be the right balance between investment and return in this relationship.

The conversation with this supplier should start with the presentation of a business case and a plan that reflects the interest of both parties. The supplier should also be made aware of the potential volume allocation for the future. The objective is to motivate the supplier to change its setup and processes. As the supplier needs to allocate core resources, the company itself also needs to dedicate core resources to improving the supplier's engineering, manufacturing, quality, or broader operational capabilities. These joint teams will align and set standards for future interaction.

Note Make sure that any changes are communicated fairly with the Develop supplier, even if—or better, especially if—changes in the original business plan or volume allocation occur. If market rumors reach the supplier about your company, the relationship will be significantly harmed.

Governance

Reach out to your in-house, cross-functional teams to identify viable candidates for being a Develop supplier. Your business needs and the strategic potential of the supplier need to be aligned.

After having handpicked the relevant supplier, a supplier meeting should be set up that encompasses not only the traditional supplier's salespeople and your company's procurement people but also other functions like engineering, manufacturing, quality and operational capabilities, and most important: the management.

When both parties have the same understanding of the future and the motivation to turn Develop into a beneficial interaction, the collaboration begins and joint teams start working. The Develop effort needs to be executed as a rigorous project with clear reporting and milestone tracking. The supplier's performance has to be monitored closely and regular biweekly meetings need to be set up.

Finally, once both parties are aiming for the same goal, performance needs to be monitored by cascading objectives down to every employee level affected by the new relationship.

Case Example

Everybody driving a car thinks about the design, the engine, the investment cost and ongoing cost, the color, and potentially about the environmental effects in terms of sustainability. Hardly any customer thinks about the steel that is in the car, even if we observe that a car consists of approximately 50–55 percent steel.

Some might say that steel cannot be the real challenge in supplier-company relationships because there are many steel producers on the market. In our estimation, there are about 130 serious suppliers. All these producers are either producing blast furnaces with iron ore, coking coal, scrap, oxygen, or alloys, or in the case of electric arc furnaces mainly with scrap. Production technology is asset intensive.

Depending on the alloys and the production process, steel types have different functions and can be used for different purposes. It is quite obvious that railway tracks, construction steel, or steel for big ships fulfill other specifications than automotive steel. Automotive steel is one of the most sophisticated types of steel. The requirements from automotive OEMs are high, as the automotive steel needs to cover the balance between elongation and yield strengths. This means, on the one hand, it should be good in terms of formability to be able to fulfill all design aspects. On the other hand, it should have enough stiffness to have a maximum of security for the driver and passengers in the car should it crash. In addition, the flat steel portion of a car requires hot-dip galvanizing, which itself requires some experience and also additional investments.

As a consequence, there are only a very few suppliers in the world that are able to fulfill automotive steel requirements and even fewer steel producers that are able to fulfill them for the premium carmakers.

China is the fastest-growing automotive market. From 2013 to 2020, the number of cars in the country is expected to double. Sales are expected to be around 30 million cars in 2020. The car manufacturers are well aware of this situation and have created new production facilities in Asia and especially in China. This will secure growth while keeping roots in the saturated markets. But the new facilities also create some challenges in terms of supply. The same growth story creating pressure on supply is true for steel. In former times, there was no supplier that was able to produce automotive steel in China.

One of the automotive companies realized this situation of constrained supply quite quickly. This was after having imported the required steel from other countries at a high cost. It then started screening the supplier market in China for steel. About 60 mills were identified that would have had the size to play in this market. A handful of suppliers had already made their first attempts to go into automotive, but without any success. The goal of the automotive OEM was to work with a Develop supplier to have a source in the country that could produce steel at Western European automotive standards. The company already had a relationship with two suppliers for certain steel parts by that time, but the satisfaction level with their overall performance was limited.

Nevertheless, top management meetings were set up with both companies to create an understanding of the future mutual benefits and how the OEM would invest its own resources to develop this supplier. A business case was created and showed that the overall tonnage in the optimistic scenario would have filled about 15 percent of the overall capacity of one of the suppliers for years. Interestingly enough, the first reaction of the companies was not excitement as was expected. China's economy was growing fast and there were significant investments in the country's infrastructure, so the companies saw their growth potential there. Besides, prices, due to supply shortages, were quite favorable. So, why add additional complexity in the process by doing hot-dip galvanizing and increased quality control?

The discussion around diversification, long-term contracts, and stable utilization that the automotive industry could bring was, however, successful and one supplier was selected for Develop. In a first step, the key resources on both sides were identified. A team was formed under the leadership of an employee who worked in former times for an EPC, or engineering procurement construction (a company that builds big plants), and afterward for a Western European steel producer, and finally settled with the Chinese supplier. Capable employees were nominated for the project team from the supplier's side. The OEM dedicated staff from engineering, the key expert from the stamping department of manufacturing, and quality-control people. In addition to its own people, the OEM also mobilized some experts from the current supplier in Europe. These experts, who came with expertise in the different steps in production, such as pig-iron production, steel milling, continuous casting, and hot- and cold-rolling mills, as well as hot-dip galvanizing were integrated. This was possible as there were no strategic plans to enter the Chinese market or vice-versa.

A project time plan was set up and executed diligently. Testing facilities and resources were made available by the OEM. After two challenging years, the first coil was delivered that was used in series production. This was a significant breakthrough for both the supplier and the OEM. Having an exclusivity agreement for a certain period of time brought significant advantage to the OEM and a solid utilization to the supplier. The investment of the OEM paid off!

Implementation Challenges at Heartland

In order to advance the implementation of SRM at Heartland, Thomas had increased the frequency of meeting Laura to weekly one-on-ones. Laura started the meeting by putting a folded page of the *Financial Times* in front of Thomas. On the page, one paragraph was bracketed.

"I read an article on the plane yesterday. It is about how carmakers deploy supplier development functions and how Japanese carmakers are leading in this sector. I was wondering if this is what we need here at Heartland to bring the Develop supplier interaction model to life."

Laura knew that deep down, Thomas was still an automotive guy and that he would share his experiences from his time working at Autowerke with passion. She would not be disappointed.

"Interesting that you are showing me this article," Thomas commented. "I was involved in upgrading Autowerke's supplier development function early in my tenure there myself. As a matter of fact, I spent two months in Japan learning from the practices of Japanese carmakers."

"What is so special about the way they do it?" Laura asked.

"Carmakers in America and in Europe have always had some kind of supplier development function, but it has largely been limited to certifying new suppliers, auditing quality, and identifying savings potential in production. Japanese carmakers have followed a higher-touch approach. They would have more and better-qualified people on the ground and actually help the suppliers with implementation teams and resident engineers. While Europeans and Americans saw supplier development mostly as programs to enforce price reductions, the Japanese saw it as an investment in the future in order to get more innovation. And this clearly paid off. There are many surveys that demonstrate the extent to which suppliers prefer Japanese carmakers over their European and American competitors. They clearly achieved a competitive advantage through improved quality and shorter time to market with better product technology."

Laura was taking notes while Thomas was speaking, "And what did you do in Japan?" she asked.

"Well, I believe that Autowerke was the first Western carmaker to fully understand the advantage the Japanese OEMs were getting out of supplier development. We entered a partnership program with the biggest Japanese carmaker in which we essentially traded our experience in diesel engine technology for their experience in supplier development. I was then part of a fairly large group of Autowerke people who spent time working in their supplier development function. If I remember correctly, we had four different teams there. One was focusing on supplier assessment, the second on interventions—meaning when something goes wrong at a supplier and you have to fix it—the third team was focusing on proactive supplier development, and the fourth one on monitoring and control. I was part of the third team, for which my subgroup focused on the Japanese way of ensuring global-production readiness at suppliers. We called it cannon launch."

"And how did you incorporate this at Autowerke?"

"Oh, this was a fairly long process—it took at least two years, I think. We started with reactive measures in order to better respond to issues our suppliers were having. Once suppliers had gained confidence in our ability to help them out, we gradually moved toward more proactive measures to help them improve their performance. Suppliers actually had to pay for our services. Initially, 75 percent of the cost was funded by Autowerke, but over time we switched to 100 percent supplier funding. This was actually very successful and our function grew to well over 200 supplier development people."

Laura appeared to be discouraged by this. "Wow, there is so much to do in parallel. How can we get anywhere close to where Autowerke is on this? We can't seriously start sending people to Japan . . . ."

"You don't need to, Laura. We can hire a couple of folks from Autowerke to be the nucleus of our own supplier development function. I know most of the key people there and I am sure that I can have a good team on board within a month or so."

Characteristics of Bail Out Suppliers

In addition to Integrate, Bail Out has the lowest number of suppliers in the SRM framework—but these suppliers are really handpicked. For a company with 1,000 suppliers, we would expect to find less than a handful of suppliers in this interaction model.

Generally speaking, suppliers in Bail Out (Figure 6-3) are highly interesting and promising. Their strategic potential is outstanding and much higher than that of the vast majority of suppliers working with the company. The products and services these suppliers provide are innovative and can be a differentiation factor for the company's position in the market.

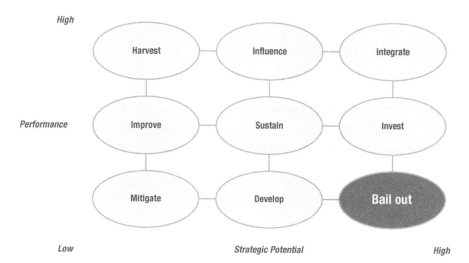

Figure 6-3. Bail Out suppliers

Nevertheless, their performance is poor. This could be based on an egregious error or a chronic problem that suddenly requires triage. Such situations can significantly jeopardize business by threatening supply or even the launch of a new product.

The immediate goal is to stabilize the supplier's performance. The long-term goal is to learn from the problem to avoid future bailouts with this supplier. It may seem counterintuitive, but this is a relationship that needs to be maintained, particularly with important suppliers. The Bail Out relationship should be brief, rare, and regarded as temporary step toward improving the overall supplier relationship.

Usually, the help is provided by you without considering what you will receive in return. Supply is threatened and you step in to correct matters. Ensuring ongoing supply is generally seen as a sufficient short-term payoff. There is not time to discuss how the help will be funded other than a quick consideration of available contractual damages.

However, "resorting to contract" immediately, when there is any form of issue with performance, does not fix the problem and is not usually an effective remedy. It also kills the relationship, and, remember that the supplier has outstanding strategic potential. Killing the relationship would not be a good long-term outcome. If there is time, instead think about more creative long-term payoffs the supplier can make in return for the help, such as exclusivity on certain products or even a part ownership share in the company. In the heat of the moment, it is difficult to think of the long-term relationship. But demonstrating your longer-term commitment will have a strong payoff.

What Kind of Behavior to Drive

The desired behavior of the Bail Out supplier is to acknowledge the severity of the situation and allow your company to intervene. To do this, the supplier needs to see the benefit it will get if it complies with the actions of the Bail Out plan.

The major investments the company makes in Bail Out suppliers will make it obvious that you have a special interest in stabilizing and strengthening the relationship. This can be communicated in a way that the supplier sees that correcting the situation will be a joint effort and also a joint benefit in the end.

This also means that the supplier should not only comply with the instructions given by the company and its potential external experts but also come up with meaningful solutions to fix shortcomings.

Note To sum up, a high ambition and motivation level of the supplier and the company, trust, and beneficial collaboration are the ingredients of success in the Bail Out interaction model.

How to Work with Bail Out Suppliers

Bailouts are expensive for everyone and time is king. This means that it is key to recognize the bailout situation immediately in order to reduce damage and to help save the relationship. It is necessary to have an open relationship with the supplier.

As there are very specific challenges that have to be resolved in bailouts, it is obvious that not everything can be fixed by the in-house experts of the company. Leading companies therefore have arrangements in place with external experts who support them in fixing problems based on their unique experience. Furthermore, using external experts will avoid bottlenecks in the company.

The company's office is not the best location for managing bailouts. Usually, the supplier's premises are the right place. This allows access to all stakeholders, access to production, and access to real-time updates. It is thus better to have boots on the ground sooner than later.

Companies often lose sight of the fact that a Bail Out supplier has high strategic potential. As a result of this, they make a major error. Once the original problem has been fixed, they sometimes feel let down by the supplier. As a result, they quickly jump to replace the supplier with a different one. This is not the right outcome. If the supplier really has high strategic potential, then the right answer is to carry on nurturing it to enable it to progress and achieve the full potential you can get from the relationship. The company's ambition for a Bail Out supplier ought to be for it to achieve its potential and ultimately be in the Critical Cluster, not be replaced.

Governance

The governance needs to recognize three key requirements: First, suppliers usually drop into Bail Out as a result of a failure. Predicting and preventing failures in advance is a crucial governance need. Second, once a supplier drops into Bail Out, the appropriate task force needs to be in place with the right governance to ensure that the issues are addressed. Third, once the issues that led to the bailout have been stabilized, then the right governance needs to be in place to prevent recurrence.

In terms of the first point, in order to recognize Bail Out situations quickly and early, there needs to be an early warning mechanism in place. The difficulty for problems with new products and new technology is that early warning mechanisms are hard to determine. One can, for example, study the trends of performance data and carry out supplier audits. Governance needs to be in place to ensure that the results of such work are reviewed across the supply base. If issues are flagged, then the appropriate guidance needs to be given to the supplier before the bailout is triggered. However, no such technique is foolproof and some bailouts will always elude the early warning system.

The second issue involves ensuring that the right governance is in place to ensure that cross-functional and external support can be deployed once a bailout is indicated. This will need to be done urgently—an important, innovative supplier with high strategic value needs help. A task force consisting of representatives of the supplier, the company, and external experts needs to be created. Both the supplier and the company need to dedicate resources. This task force drives the performance improvement in a project type of setting. A kind of war room setup enables the joint team to execute the project and to make the improvements transparent. A joint steering committee will need to be in place to govern the work of the task force and provide an escalation point. It is also crucial to avoid encumbering the task force with commercial or contractual topics. Allow the task force to fix things. Deal with any commercial concerns separately and at a steering committee level.

In the third requirement, once the situation is stabilized, the task force can be unwound and the governance revert to a more business-as-usual approach, with the supplier being able to manage its own affairs without detailed day-to-day intervention on your part. There is a balance to strike here between the risks of unwinding the task force too quickly vs. the more desirable choice to revert to the normal state of affairs. Agree on a joint plan for reverting to normal. Review progress. Take a gradual approach and be prepared to step in again as you slowly wind down the task force. As you do this, make sure that you put in place the right governance measures that will help to prevent recurrence of the issues that gave rise to the bailout in the first place. Assess the risks of recurrence. Be prepared to put in place more detailed ongoing oversight than may be your norm. But, be careful too. The supplier needs to stand on its own two feet. Do not over compensate for past failings. Base your approach on a true view of the real, not perceived, risks. Managed well, the supplier will be on track to continue as a valued member of your supply base.

Case Example

Most people relate battle tanks to war and many things that are not really nice. We should not overlook the fact that battle tanks are also used for peacekeeping and for the self-defense of countries. We are going to come back to this point.

Despite all the bad feelings that come along with speaking about tanks, we have to admit that they are fascinating from an engineering point of view. Depending on the type, these vehicles have a double-digit tonnage, are able to drive over 100 kilometers per hour, can swim, can crawl after swimming in muddy shores, and can climb mountains with inclines of up to 70 degrees. These are indeed quite-impressive specifications.

Nevertheless, the core pieces of a battle tank are engine, steel, electronics, and protection systems. While the first three categories are supplied by big players like Cummins, MTU, SSAB, and others, the protection systems could be supplied by quite an innovative player.

A very successful company in the land-defense sector got a new contract from the Ministry of Defense from a specific country. While the company had a proven protection system from a well-established supplier, R & D was working to gain a competitive advantage by enabling a new protection system for the tank. R & D was working very intensively, in particular with one supplier that had a completely new technology. Tests were performed in top-secret locations, and waste was eliminated so that nobody could have any hints of this new technology. Neither sales, nor engineering, nor production had any doubts that this new technology was leading the market. No other supplier than this one could bring the same reduced weight to the protection system by increasing the degree of protection. Impressions on the overall setup of the supplier were also good. The client, a national Ministry of Defense, was also confident in this new technology and the client's engineers were excited about it. This new technology was also one of the winning factors for the overall contract, a clear strategic advantage for the company.

After the preparation phase, production started and suppliers made their first deliveries. Beside the normal challenges in a project-based business in this sector, the new and highly praised protection system brought severe problems. The quality was not consistent, the deliveries were delayed, and the operational performance overall was a disaster.

The company had some experience with low-performing suppliers and reacted in the right way. A task force was established and sent immediately to the supplier. It was not an easy step given the fact that the big contract had to be managed, but with the necessity and also the strategic advantage, the management freed up resources. Already, after the first poor-quality deliveries, they had their feet on the ground and worked together with the supplier, which fully realized that these operational issues could wipe it out of the market.

The task force supported the supplier to bring the new innovative technology to a consistent quality level and enabled the supplier to manage its operations professionally. This company's relationship with the supplier got very tense over the period of the bailout. Nowadays, the company is highly profitable, and, after a period of exclusivity, opened the market to others, too. A nice unexpected outcome: this supplier always offers its innovations first to the company that helped it in fixing its problem—a continuous strategic advantage.

Heartland: Calbury Races Ahead

Thomas was in a rueful mood. Laura sat down. He opened up his iPad and handed it to her and asked her to look at the screen. "Calbury sure is doing well with that 'Taste Fresh Longer' packaging that it sources from Marshfield. See this announcement here of the extra sales that the company is driving from it? Well, the company's not just making extra sales on the product but both companies are also making really nice margins."

"I saw that earlier as well," said Laura. "The joint venture that Marshfield and Calbury set up has a patent on it, as you know. They are really not interested in making it available to anyone else."

"I heard talk that they might be making it available soon," Thomas offered.

"So far, it is just rumors," Laura speculated. "I think what they will do is make a less-sophisticated version of the packaging available more widely. They are worried about competition concerns, and Marshfield does have an interest in driving more volume than they get purely from Calbury. But the most sophisticated formulation of the packaging will remain exclusive to Calbury we hear—at least for the foreseeable future."

"Right now, our response is to work with another company to develop an alternative that does not infringe the patent," suggested Thomas. "That will take time and be expensive. Or we just hope that Marshfield's competitors will do something anyway. In the meantime, our retail customers are keener to push Calbury brands in what is one of our prime categories. Not a great place to be in."

"You know," said Laura, "things could have been very different."

"How?" asked Thomas. "Marshfield has been quite a peripheral supplier to us for quite a while. We have only kept buying the product that we needed for logistical reasons, really. But the company has been one of Calbury's major suppliers for a long time. Calbury did a lot to build the relationship and ecosystem that we are now seeing in place. Our failure has not been not doing the same thing with someone else."

"You know it was not always like that though, Thomas. A few years before you joined from Autowerke as CPO, the company was actually seen as a key supplier. I remember that it supplied our Italian plant. It was really significant."

"I did not know that. What happened?"

"We had the great 'ripping of film' drama about five years ago."

"I did hear someone refer to that," said Thomas. "What has that got to do with it?"

"Well, Marshfield was our biggest film supplier. You know how production people are with film. A lot of the specifications are custom-made and take practice. Accordingly, they are hard to codify. The production people hate changes, even if they might be beneficial."

"Right, tell me about it," said Thomas.

"OK, so Marshfield came to us with a great idea to make the film stronger and even more lustrous to the touch while still being thin. It would make the product look better. It was an interesting innovation, but our production people were reluctant to do it. It would be slightly cheaper, but that was not a real reason to do it and Procurement had no real power at that time anyway. However, the fact that it made the product look better meant that it got support from Marketing. So, it was agreed to do a trial on the new film in one of our plants—the one in Ulm."

"That was a brave thing to do, then," said Thomas.

"At the time, it came to be seen as something quite beyond 'brave.' It was set up as a pilot, but Marshfield had all sorts of problems with the new film. First, it started to break in our machines, even though it was supposed to be stronger. That was, in reality, partly our fault due to how we were running the machines. Then, Marshfield had problems making enough of it in the right quality and consistency. We did not have a supplier development team back then, but we did put some production engineers in there to help sort out the problems. It was a bit like closing the door after the horse had bolted."

"I see," said Thomas. "So, it was a bit of a panic?"

"Oh yes. Many people bore the scars. We got it fixed in the end and no actual product was affected by the problems. Also, the production schedule was not really hit because we had inventory anyway. We always had lots of inventory of film in those days, whether we needed it or not."

"What lessons were learned?" asked Thomas.

Laura laughed. "Not the lessons we should have learned. What we should have learned is that for a product change like that to be successful and for real innovation to take place, you need to carry out joint planning up-front and collaborate. We did not do that. We just went into crisis mode at the first sign of trouble."

"What else happened?"

"That is the real tragedy. We blamed the supplier for all the problems. In reality, the fault was on both sides. And, the company was genuinely trying to give us first access to an interesting innovation! For all of its pains, it ended being tagged as an unreliable supplier. We started to move business away from the company. Everyone started to see awarding business to Marshfield as career limiting. So, it became less important. It works both ways, of course. We became less important to the company and it built their relationship with Calbury. Nobody stopped to think that perhaps Marshfield had something genuinely different to offer us. They just focused on the ripping-of-film drama."

"And the rest is history," said Thomas. "Calbury reaps the benefits of our shortsightedness."

"It gets more tragic though, would you believe?" said Laura.

"How can it get more tragic than that?" inquired Thomas. He leaned forward to concentrate. This was really was turning into quite a revelatory discussion.

"Well," said Laura, "there are rumors in the marketplace. People are saying that the know-how that Marshfield gleaned to create the Taste Fresh Longer line came as a direct result of the ripping-of-film debacle."

"What? Seriously?!" commented Thomas, surprised.

"Yes. They learned a lot about the chemical properties of how to make different types of film from the incident. Also, our troubleshooting with them at an operational level was highly successful. They learned the additional lesson that collaboration with key customers on product innovation can be beneficial. According to our own rumor mill, they did try to do that with us. But, of course, we were not listening and they had written us off. They turned instead to working with Calbury. Although it took a few years, this led directly to the innovation that is now causing us so much irritation."

Thomas took his iPad back from Laura. "We really need to avoid similar debacles like this in the future. Let's learn the lessons."

Problematics: Handle with Care

In this chapter, we have described the three interaction models that make up the Problematics, or problem children. As we have seen, these suppliers should constitute far fewer than 10 percent of your total supply base. This is just as well because in all cases performance is poor and serious fixes are needed. Where strategic potential is low, you should not incur effort to make the fix but replace the supplier after giving it sufficient opportunity to improve. In other cases, where strategic potential is higher, you should incur effort to nurture the supplier toward greater things.

We will turn our attention in Chapter 7 to address the suppliers that are already capable of these greater things. These are the suppliers in the Critical Cluster—the very small number of suppliers from which you can access true innovation and the ones to which you really want to devote the majority of your attention.

The "Critical Cluster"

Driving Behavior to Get Results

Our tour of the different clusters is completed with the "Critical Cluster." We finish here because this is the area where the most important suppliers will be located. These are suppliers that can contribute to competitive advantage and where the relationship needs special nurturing. It is from these suppliers that you will get the most innovation and risk mitigation.

The secret sauce to making this relationship model work is to establish trust with these suppliers. Failure to create the necessary level of trust is probably the number one reason so few companies create such deep relationships with these suppliers. Free markets and competition encourage companies to be secretive and protect their competitive advantage while it lasts. Many are afraid they will lose it if they get too comfortable with their suppliers, which in many cases also cater to the company's biggest competitors. But establishing deep trust can work, and we are strong believers that every company that wants to can reap the benefits of a close relationship with the right suppliers.

Think of one of the world's most secretive consumer-electronics companies, notorious for keeping its newest products secret even to most of its own employees. Yet part of its secret sauce is working very closely with key partners that help develop, test, and manufacture most of its products. The relationship is built on strong mutual dependence and deep trust going beyond cultural barriers, which has vaulted both companies to the top levels in their industry.

Most companies won't have that level of trust with suppliers when starting with SRM. The way forward is to focus on the fundamentals of the interaction model first, and then develop trust through time as the relationship deepens and evolves. Using the concrete actions of collaboration as stepping stones serves to build that trust. Lastly, being transparent with the supplier in applying the interaction model is a way to engender trust with it.

Let's look at each of the three types of suppliers in the Critical Cluster in depth.

Characteristics of Influence Suppliers

Very few suppliers will fit the Influence model (Figure 7-1). To do so, they would have to perform very well in all regards. You could say that those in this model deliver nearly perfect products or services. What sets them apart is that they offer the potential for innovation when you work with them jointly to develop new products or services. This factor shapes your relationship with them.

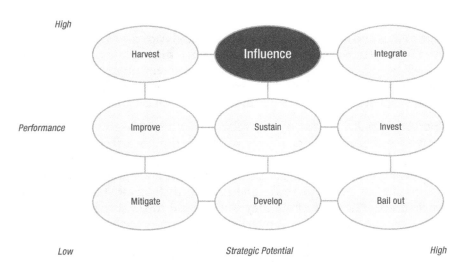

Figure 7-1. Influence suppliers on the strategy/performance axes

Compared to Integrate suppliers, companies cannot build lasting competitive advantage with Influence suppliers. This is because they do not offer the full long-term and all-embracing partnership that is required to steal a march on your competitors over the long term. These suppliers often dominate an industry, as they are among the critical few that a company and its competitors rely on. They supply key technologies or services that define the industry's standard and their share of wallet is likely to be very high. To provide such a high level of innovation, they often invest heavily in development or capital equipment cost. As a result, they will often favor scale over exclusivity in order to amortize the up-front investments. In turn, they do not favor any one customer, and, in the case of monopolistic suppliers, are required by law not to do so. At times, you may be able to achieve limited exclusivity on specific innovations as a launch customer in return for assisting with the upfront development. However, over time, the Influence supplier will certainly seek to make the innovation available more widely. This is a reality that you need to recognize.

So, you get cutting-edge service and innovative products. The downside, of course, is that it is nearly impossible to outpace your competition forever when you work with these suppliers. What's more, mismanage this relationship, and you could alienate these suppliers enough that you fall behind the competitors that are better at handling their relationship with the same supplier.

What Kind of Behavior to Drive

The preferred behavior from an Influence supplier is to be able to affect its innovation roadmaps and be the first to the market with new technology. You will, at least, want to get some level of preferential treatment as well. The essential ingredient to the relationship is building trust and an incentive structure that will motivate the supplier to open up. The supplier has to see the type of competencies you bring to the table and the benefit in working with you in particular. You need to put yourself in its shoes to truly understand what drives it. As a highly innovative technology company, it may seek a company with a strong sales channel to quickly position its products and drive fast growth. Or it may be after specific market segments in which it is not yet established or that it sees as being of strategic importance. Then again, it may just need a sufficient initial order to jump over the internal hurdle to get the final "go" to develop a new product or service.

An Influence supplier may aspire to become an Integrate supplier with your organization, but that will only happen in very few selected cases, as it would mean deprioritizing or even ignoring other customers. This may happen in the case of a nascent technological innovation that presents a high, risky bet and where a powerful ecosystem of specific customers and buyers provides the right mix of competencies to make it work. The company is hoping to get as much out of the relationship as you are. Once the technology becomes more mature, the relationship might drift back to Influence, but this may take several years or product and service generations to come.

On the other hand, the supplier may fall short in terms of future innovations and—even while maintaining the same flawless performance levels—might move back to being a Harvest supplier. This will happen, for instance, when there is a jump in the technology curve and the supplier has missed the innovation window either as leader or follower.

How to Work with Influence Suppliers

As with most relationships in life, good timing and regular communication are critical for capitalizing on opportunities with Influence suppliers. You want to set the expectation up-front that it is necessary to have access to their product, technology, process, and innovation roadmaps. Evaluate the supplier for opportunities that you can tap into or even areas that could provide limited exclusivity. Request ongoing feedback on how your company's actions and plans dovetail with its own for mutual advantage, and then negotiate competitive pricing accordingly. And don't be shy and stop here; rather, go further to also align on strategy and dedicate resources to generate a sustained competitive advantage.

Influence relationships can consume a substantial amount of resources, so you need to make the investment pay off by encouraging confidence in each other's plans. In case of interesting new product technologies, you might want to become a launch customer to gain first-mover advantage and to get preferential treatment over the lifetime of the product.

Note Influence relationships can be time-consuming, so make the investment pay off. Ask to become a launch customer for an innovation, for example. That can give you that coveted "first mover" advantage, as well as goodwill you can capitalize upon later.

As a launch customer, you will be first to recognize the potential future strategic value of the new product or service, and must often be willing to write a check several months if not years in advance before actually seeing the result. But keep in mind that Influence suppliers are not just looking for resources—if that were the only thing they were interested in, they could go elsewhere. They are mostly looking for a sales channel to find first users of their innovation right after the product launch. Becoming a launch customer enables exactly that: It provides a convincing sales channel and commitment to buy sufficient ramp-up volume. In return, the supplier will get preferential treatment and even a say in the product- or service-development process. This can be valuable; the company may suggest certain features that would otherwise not have been considered by your development team. In many cases, there will be an exclusive relationship for a certain amount of time after the product launch. It may not last long, though. To drive improvements and stay competitive in the market, the supplier will go after scale and start offering the same product or service to other customers. As a launch customer, you may neverthe-less still receive special treatment in terms of higher price discounts, better product or service support, and committer capacity, something that can be especially critical in times of supply disruptions.

Governance

These relationships are based on mutual trust, so you want to make sure the supplier understands the importance of the relationship to you. Nominate a sponsor for the relationship on both sides, someone with suf-ficient political weight to drive the alignment of priorities for new product or service development. Mutual teams could be built to drive develop-ment of future products. The supplier may even send dedicated people to join your development teams and allow for real-time feedback loops.

Typically, you should expect a series of regular formal executive reviews, at least quarterly, that focus on identifying future opportunities and review-ing progress in collaborative innovation efforts. In addition, plan to hold a series of informal meetings to strengthen the relationship at all levels and across different stakeholder groups.

Case Example #1

Let's look at an example for Influence from the commercial aircraft indus-try, which is an extremely complex industry. It has high barriers to entry and it is capital intensive, with companies realizing profits only after a long time. With only a few manufacturers of aircraft—even just two in the long-distance aircraft market—the airlines will never be able to get exclu-sive deals from any of them. So there is a strong incentive on the airline side to gain access to new aircraft development as soon as possible and get the starting advantage over other airlines.

In the late 1980s, the aircraft maker Airbus started to think of develop-ing a new ultra high-capacity airliner to break the dominance of Boeing's 747 as the only true high-capacity, long-distance aircraft. Developing new technologies and designing aircraft is a long-term process with significant financial risk; the development costs of designing a new airplane are in the billions. Singapore Airlines recognized the opportunity by building a strong relationship with Airbus. Both sides had high win-win expectations for their cooperation. The airline wanted first-mover advantage as the launch customer, but it had a primary interest in influencing the develop-ment process, specifically the design of the passenger cabin. The aircraft producer was given security through a committed initial order from one of the leading global airlines with a convincing marketing arm that would quickly bring other customers on board.

Singapore Airlines capitalized on the possibility of influencing the design process of the cabin by redefining the flying experience. The new first class is not even called that anymore—the company describes it as "beyond first class." The luxurious suites are targeted at passengers who do not want to compromise on either sleeping or the seating and working experience while in air. Each "suite" has a full-size mattress, sliding doors, and pull-down windows. It more resembles an old, classy train cabin than an airplane seat, and it sets a new standard for luxury in commercial aircraft. The flight attendants actually walk between walls, not seats. If you want to work on your computer, you can connect it to the large screen hanging on the wall of the suite. If you want to dine with another passenger, you can do that as well. There is even a suite with a double bed that the airline coined as "honeymooners' suite." This clearly propelled the airline to the top as the trendsetter for luxury air travel. The airline also cares for its staff and has further improved the area flight attendants work in. Several additional comfort features have been implemented for both pilots and the crew.

Singapore Airlines had great success as the launch customer for the new jumbo jet. It significantly expanded its brand value, customer base, and new services. In less than one-and-a-half years, the one-millionth passenger flew with Singapore Airlines on the new A380 aircraft. A big marketing effort, followed by extensive media coverage, turned the airline into the best-known airline carrier. Especially successful was a charity auction on eBay, in which passengers bought seats paying between $560 and $100,380 for the first-scheduled flight of the aircraft. That turned into a huge marketing success. To commemorate the inaugural flight, passengers received a personalized certificate showing they were part of the first historic flight. The airline also profited from the early stage of cooperation by being able to develop a new customer experience with the newly defined business-suite class influencing the aircraft's interior design.

Airbus's advantages from the early-stage cooperation turned into a big success as well, as they not only heard the voice of the customer through the entire product development process but also profited from free media coverage. And even more important, the buying commitment from one of the largest and most admired airlines positively influenced buying decisions from other airlines.

Case Example #2

The same kind of close working relationship paid off for the transportation authority of London, a city which already had a highly modern fleet of off-the-shelf buses in operation. In this case, it wanted a new bus that was especially tailored to London's operating conditions. It also wanted the new bus to become as iconic on the city's streets as the classic open-platform Routemaster design of the 1950s had been. In short, London desired a bus that would be an emblem for the city. In 2010, it chose the outline design via a public competition and selected Wrightbus for the manufacture and detailed design. The detailed styling was then produced through close collaboration with Heatherwick Studio.

The suppliers created a unique vehicle that meets the specific needs of London's ridership with full wheelchair and pram accessibility, a hybrid electric- and diesel-power engine, and an aluminum frame, making it one of the most environmentally friendly buses in the world. The iconic feature of a rear open platform enabling hop-on, hop-off operation when a conductor is present was preserved. Building on the success of its namesake predecessor, the new Routemaster features asymmetric glass swoops as its signature "futuristic" styling feature.

Inspired by the classic Routemaster, the transportation authority and bus manufacturer developed the first bus in more than 50 years to be designed specifically for London's streets. This joint supplier relationship successfully introduced this cutting-edge vehicle on the city's streets and produced the largest order for hybrid buses in Europe. The transportation authority has had significant influence on the bus manufacturer's product roadmap and the design of the bus. While the bus is quite specific to London, it will be available for the broader customer base interested in purchase of double-decker city buses.

Collaboration Pays Off for Heartland

Laura was musing over the missed opportunity that Marshfield had represented as she walked into the office at Fort Wayne one morning. There was a spring in her step, though. She was wondering whether today would represent redemption for Heartland Consolidated Industries and a tangible outcome from TrueSRM that would really be "something big." For today was the culmination of many months of really focused work between a cross-functional Heartland team and Caledonian Packaging, a packaging-industry competitor of Marshfield. It was the day that both companies would make a formal announcement of a major new innovation into the market. The innovation was being made by Caledonian. Heartland was committing resources and funds. In return for the resources and funds, Heartland was made the launch customer. Analysts, customers, and press representatives had been invited. The innovation was expected to have a major impact on both Heartland's and Caledonian's respective revenue and stock prices. The presentation really needed to go well. The atmosphere in Fort Wayne was electric. The spring in Laura's step was tinged with trepidation.

The story had started six months before. Caledonian was a long-term supplier to Heartland. It had reaped much of the benefit from the long-term decline in Marshfield serving as a Heartland supplier following the great "ripping film" debacle. Yet there was a sense that Caledonian had grown a little complacent at Heartland. Nobody could remember the last great innovation that Caledonian had introduced. It was not clear to anyone, in fact, that they "did" innovation at all. However, they were seen as safe, their film and other materials worked in Heartland's machines, and no one was likely to get fired for using them. Heartland was also not sure that it even needed packaging innovation, especially in the post–ripping film era.

As we have seen, this apparent complacency on both sides was dramatically shaken by the "Tastes Fresh Longer" innovation. Both Heartland and Caledonian were embarrassed. The initial reaction was, as might be expected, one of mutual recrimination. Both Laura and Thomas had attended a meeting to which they had urgently summoned Calum Drummond, the Caledonian CEO, and senior members of his team. This had been a very difficult meeting. The Heartland executives started out by berating the Caledonian people for being complacent and not bringing anything to the table. At first, Calum had stayed silent, while his colleagues politely listened to Heartland and showed contrition.

However, the meeting turned ugly when Heartland's CFO, Garner, intervened and commented, "You know, I really wonder whether Caledonian should be one of our suppliers going forward."

Calum was a feisty Scotsman. There was no way he was going to tolerate any more one-sided abuse. "A customer gets the behavior it deserves," he contested. "You have wanted safety and security for the past three years. Everything you have told us has to do with 'Please make sure there are no more ripping film sagas.' We have done what you asked. You have shown no interest in any innovation that we have shown you. You reject everything that is new. The 'no more ripping films' instruction is engraved on our hearts. Now, when you are caught out, you have the gall to blame us. I am shocked at what I am hearing today. Do you want to fix things or just sit here kicking my team? I have had enough . . . ."

Calum motioned to leave.

Thomas, who had been silent, raised his hand to speak. "Calum, let's fix things. I hear you. I think we have all got a little emotional today. Let's have a short break to stretch our legs." He summoned Calum and the two of them stepped out of the room together and walked toward Thomas's office.

"Thank you for pushing back, Calum," said Thomas. "That is always hard for a supplier to do. My team were maybe a little out of order but you can appreciate the emotion this has aroused."

"I do," said Calum.

They entered Thomas's office. "So tell me," inquired Thomas, "What are these innovations we keep rejecting? I am intrigued."

Calum had a seat. "Well," he said. "There are many examples. But the one we are really proud of is that we came up with an idea for a film that changes color. It changes color if the product has at any time been kept at the wrong temperature. You know, so many foods can spoil and the end customer will just take into consideration the final temperature. But, a guarantee of the correct temperature right through the supply chain really is something else." Calum was getting quite animated. "We think some retailers may not like it but the premium ones will embrace it to prove their credentials. Then, the rest will have no choice but to follow."

"When did you talk to us about it?" asked Thomas.

"Oh, a couple of months ago."

"And you have not gone elsewhere with it yet?" Thomas inquired.

"No. Given that Calbury works so much with Marshfield, we prefer not to take it there. And, we really feel we need to work closely with a customer to perfect it. It's exciting but a bit untried, so ideally we would like to see a launch customer prepared to invest in it. We have been hoping that would be Heartland."

"You know, Calum, you and I should meet more," smiled Thomas. "I think that together we might be able to cut through some of the red tape on things like this."

"Music to my ears," said Calum.

They returned to the conference room. The air had cleared a bit. The other team members were talking about the color-changing film, too. One of the Heartland people had remembered it from the discussion two months before. With a slight steer from Thomas and Calum, the meeting moved from a recrimination session into "How to compete with Calbury and Marshfield." The plan was borne to co-commercialize the color-changing film. Both parties committed resources and investment. They also agreed to act rapidly.

Some months later, Laura found herself walking with trepidation into the presentation of the formal launch of the color-changing film to an awaiting world. She took her seat next to Scarlet, the CMO. This event was sufficiently high profile that both Thomas and Calum were the key presenters, rather than the functional leaders. They needn't have worried though. The presentation was received incredibly well. The news went viral within minutes of it being announced.

That evening, Chuck Evans, the CEO of Calbury, was asked for a comment by a business reporter as he attended a reception. All he was able to muster was, "No comment." Thomas chuckled when he read that in the news the next day. He could not resist picking the phone up to talk to Calum. By now, they were on very easy speaking terms.

Characteristics of Invest Suppliers

Suppliers that fall into the Invest interaction model (Figure 7-2) provide a portfolio of products or services that could become game changing. Their strategic potential is very high. They offer great ideas and innovations, but then they stumble in some basic areas, such as providing continuous supply or consistent quality. These capability gaps limit the potential to achieve truly game-changing moves with them. Ultimately, they could reach Integrate status—but their potential for this rests on the relationship you build with them now and the extent to which they respond. Typically, exclusivity is not really important but rather the willingness of both parties to cooperate and drive capability improvements.

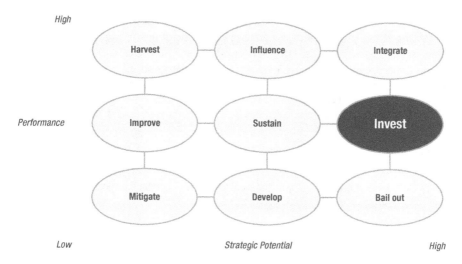

Figure 7-2. Invest suppliers on the strategy/performance axes

The Invest model can also include investment in development of new product or service offerings. It can be investment in new material or production technology. In some industries, such as aerospace, it is common for customers and suppliers to participate in new projects via risk- and revenue-sharing partnerships. Both parties contribute to development costs and share the returns. Typically, new programs require a major development cost and suppliers have some of the key expertise that is needed to support it. Original equipment manufacturers (OEM) will expect that suppliers commit both expertise and capital to finance the cost. The basic principle applied is that suppliers that have to make the most up-front investment are entitled to a proportional share of the revenue as the project realizes its goals. Revenue will be earned over the period that could be as long as 30 years, and profit increases toward the end of the product life cycle once both parties start selling spare parts. This illustrates a very nontraditional customer-supplier relationship. Both parties invest heavily in new product development, and if they fail, they fail together. The supplier has a strong incentive to make the investment. Often this is accompanied by additional investment on the OEM side to ensure that suppliers deliver the expected performance levels.

What Kind of Behavior to Drive

Ideally, an Invest supplier will aspire to Integrate status and will invest with you in building capabilities to achieve this title. It is OK or even desired for the supplier to be bullish about its future with you. But, it also needs to be able to look into the mirror and recognize the necessity that it improves.

Provided this is the case, we recommend nurturing the relationship by investing time, money, and resources in developing the supplier's capabilities to meet your needs. The best candidates will make capability building a top priority. Be forewarned, however, that some suppliers may spurn the help, believing that you are attempting to make them "captive" and to cut them off from wider market opportunities.

Note Some suppliers may not appreciate their "Invest" categorization. They may feel that getting into bed with you now cuts off other opportunities down the road. In other words, what looks like a golden opportunity to you may not look so enticing from their point of view. You may need to make a good argument to attract their cooperation.

The capability building will follow an aggressive improvement plan with a clearly defined target set and a roadmap on how to get there. To ensure success, the supplier's leadership has to share this vision and cascade it through the organization. The purpose, or "Why?" for the capability building has to be clear. In order not to get off the path, these changes must be pushed with a high sense of urgency. You will also need to apply steady pressure. Identify tenacious change agents in the Invest supplier's organization that will take the messages and influence the naysayer to remove the roadblocks for improvement. As you progress along the path, document improvements and provide areas for growth to the supplier so that it sees the return on the investment.

How to Work with Invest Suppliers

In some ways, the Invest model can be likened to a wedding engagement. You need to strike the right balance between nurturing the supplier, engendering trust, and overcoming fears of "capture."

A transparent business case that both parties buy into will help alleviate supplier hesitancy. It should present a compelling return on investment for both parties. To make this work, you need to know what the current pain points are for your internal stakeholders—not just Procurement, but also Engineering, Product Marketing, Quality, and others. And to get your investment priorities right, you need to understand the overall impact, reviewing with the supplier the timetable to build capabilities in line with your expectations. In this model, it is essential that you stick to your commitments in order to reduce the risk to the supplier.

Implementation can be performed by the supplier alone if it has sufficient capabilities in-house; if not, you can assist by temporarily assigning your own resources or by engaging external help. Often these relationships will require you to have boots on the ground, meaning you send your own resources to the supplier's site, be it an engineering group or a factory where it makes the products. This simplifies collaboration, especially when investing in making something new.

Governance

The Invest interaction model means that both parties have a vested interest in the collaboration. Building a supplier's competencies is given the highest priority and both groups are focused on making the investment pay off. Typically, a joint steering committee is established to govern the process and track progress. Given the close cooperation, it is important that you also clearly define the parties' respective roles and responsibilities to limit confusion.

Case Example #1

Let's look at an example from the consumer electronics industry, which is known for having all of the production outsourced to contract-manufacturing partners. Relationships with suppliers need to be carefully managed to be able to deliver products to the market. The industry is further characterized by short product life cycles, with many products sold for only 12 or 18 months. One of the world's largest consumer electronics companies, Apple, outpaced its competition by focusing on technological innovation, design, and corporate leadership. As with many other OEMs, Apple sold all of its in-house manufacturing capacity in the 1990s, and it has relied since then solely on outsourced manufacturers.

Following the huge success of its products, Apple decided to consolidate its supply base of contract manufacturers (CM) to allow for better control of product cost, lead times, and quality. One particular CM, Hon Hai Precision Industry (better known as Foxconn), had the potential to become Apple's single most important contractor due to its flexibility in following the company's guidelines. The resulting success of Foxconn in terms of cost-effectiveness and market flexibility depends largely on Apple's strategy of investing heavily in the relationship. In its megafactories, Foxconn was able to reorganize production lines, and their staffing and logistics, in a very short time at the lowest cost. At the same time, they followed Apple's rigorous specifications of price, product quality, and time-to-market.

Let's look more closely at examples of how Apple invested in Foxconn to increase its performance. First of all, Apple's teams of engineers and supply chain managers were sent as a task force to Foxconn's factories in an effort to improve production and quality control. The dispatched teams worked together with Foxconn as long as needed to resolve any manufacturing and supply chain issues. The way they worked together was as one team with clearly defined roles. In addition to investing resources, Apple decided to invest billions of dollars in a production line. A look into its balance sheets, specifically at the data for machine and equipment expenditure, reveals that there is a consistent pattern of investment in equipment and tools installed in its supply base. The technology giant has clearly been pursuing a strategic goal to extend control over the supply chain. The expenditure has increased to several billion dollars per year, and the bulk of the spending is on product tooling and manufacturing process equipment. It has been rumored that in one year, Apple has invested ten times as much in computer numerical control (CNC) machines and tooling installed at Foxconn's factories than it has in its own retail stores. By revolutionizing the use of CNC machining and anodizing in the computer electronics industry, the company has been able to offer very unique product designs as one of its major market differentiators. The advantage is a single-piece unibody design, making the housing seamless and beautiful, which is possible because the CNC solution allows the number of build parts to be reduced dramatically in the case of a unibody notebook chassis. The holes can also be produced to a much tighter tolerance than if they were simply molded into the part. The whole assembly process is also made easier and the manufacturing becomes closer to full automation because CNC machines run in lights-off factories. The latest example of an innovation is Apple investing in robots and placing them in Foxconn's megafactories. By investing so much in robotics, the company will retain its leadership in manufacturing technology, product quality, and worker efficiency for many more years.

Case Example #2

Another example of the Invest interaction model can be found in the automotive industry. As electric cars are becoming mainstream, many companies and groups of engineers are looking for ways to establish themselves in the industry. They are reshaping the mechanics of the automobile, as many old paradigms do not hold any more. If we wanted to make a bold claim, we could go as far as comparing an electric car to an oversized cell phone: in the end, it is primarily a huge battery and the electronics to operate it. To design a mainstream electric car, you need a more optimal mileage range. Some of the improvements carmakers are pushing include improving the weight of the car (the lighter the better to minimize energy consumption), improving the aerodynamics of the car, and extending battery life by providing the ability to recharge while driving and larger and lighter batteries.

BMW decided to bet on the use of carbon fibers to significantly reduce the weight of the car. Based on initial design estimates, the company expected that using carbon fibers would reduce the weight of a small electric car, designed for use in the cities, by 500–800 pounds. Today, most cars in general are made of steel or aluminum, and carbon frames are half the weight of steel and two-thirds the weight of aluminum. With much less weight in the car body, BMW decided that it could put a much larger battery inside to provide greater mileage. Having very limited experience with the material, which was until then used for some high-end sports and racing cars, this was a risky bet. What was needed was a supplier with relevant experience and a willingness to make the technology affordable for mass production. The company reached out to SGL Carbon, one of the world's leading manufacturers of products using carbon fiber. The manufacturer recognized the value of the opportunity and decided to participate in an investment in a state-of-the-art factory in Moses Lake, Washington, that would produce carbon fibers. This location was picked for its cheap and readily available clean hydropower from the dams of the Columbia River. The production of carbon fibers is the most energy-consuming process in the entire value chain, so this had huge cost implications.

The joint partners set up an entire value chain process: the raw materials would be imported from a Japanese supplier and the spools of carbon fiber from Moses Lake would then be shipped to plants in Germany to be woven into fabric and later molded into parts at BMW's factory. Factories were set up to mass-produce the ultra-lightweight body components from carbon fiber-reinforced plastics and make the new technology affordable. Indeed, this joint venture is expected to set a precedent for the use of carbon fiber in mass-produced vehicles, a milestone for the automotive industry.

A Challenge for Heartland

Despite the air-conditioning running at full speed, Laura felt perspiration building up on her forehead. When Tracey Lin, the head of Heartland's North American Food Division, had asked her to support a request for benchmarking procurement with EATing, the largest high-end grocery chain, she had assumed it would be a walk in the park. Granted, there had been some hesitation at the prospect of helping a customer become smarter in Procurement, but Thomas had quickly waived concerns with, "If we don't do it, somebody else will. And we have more to gain than lose from opening up to them."

What Laura had not expected, though, was the aggressiveness with which the EATing people had approached the benchmarking.

They had sent a long-and-detailed agenda of what they wanted to see and they had proposed breakout groups to discuss certain topics more in depth. Then they wanted the breakout groups to be coheaded by EATing and Heartland representatives. When it turned out that most of the EATing representatives were former consultants from top firms, Laura started to have doubts as to whether her own people would be an appropriate match. After all, her program to upgrade the overall caliber of Procurement talent had only just started.

Today, Laura had to face a visit from EATing to discuss the benchmarking. Their delegation turned out to be overseen by EATing's head of category management, Spike Turner. That, in turn, made the visit a top affair at Heartland. After all, EATing was the company's second-largest retail customer, and Spike had never visited Heartland before. Even Tracey had second thoughts.

She had said to Laura, "I hope this is not about them assessing the effectiveness of our procurement. The last thing we want is for them to impose an improvement program on us and then squeeze us for the benefits." After all, EATing had a reputation for being exceptionally ruthless with suppliers.

The meeting with EATing turned out to be even more challenging than expected. Laura's presentation on Heartland Procurement best practices clearly had failed to impress despite her best efforts. Her war stories about introducing cost regression analysis to Heartland had been interrupted by Spike saying: "If I remember correctly, we introduced statistical tools to category management back in the early '90s. There was a golden opportunity when the stock market was down and we could snap up some analysts from Wall Street for cheap. Retail is a cutthroat business with razor-thin margins, you know. Obviously, Heartland is far more comfortable than we are." It took a couple of seconds for Laura to compose herself after this. She knew how to deal with high-ranking supplier executives and board members, but this was different. If this meeting went sour, a lot of revenue would be at stake.

"Spike, I sense that you are not getting what you are looking for out of this meeting. Please help me to better understand, what would make you deem the trip to Fort Wayne worthwhile?"

Before Tracey could say anything, the executive responded: "OK, let me be frank with you. We have run out of ideas on what to do on the procurement end of category management. We know for sure that we at EATing are better than all our competitors, yet our margins are still disappointing. So we have turned to our three biggest suppliers for inspiration. You are actually the last one we are talking to. We have drawn blanks in the first two meetings and quite frankly, this looks like another one. Don't get me wrong, what you are doing here is all very good and admirable and so on, but there is nothing exceptional, nothing we can transfer to EATing. So for the sake of your time and our time, it might be best to wrap up."

Without hesitating for a second, Laura knew what to do. "Well, there is one more thing that I have not talked about. It is brand new and we have not fully gotten our heads around it. We call it TrueSRM." She then went on to explain the story of the voyage of discovery that Heartland had embarked on, including some of the key successes like the collaboration with Caledonian. The EATing delegation asked lots of questions and the discussion quickly veered away from the presentation slides in a highly positive way. The discussion extended way beyond the agreed time.

It was not obvious at the time, but ultimately, that day—and specifically that discussion of TrueSRM—would come to be marked in the annals of Heartland as the day that transformed the relationship with EATing. Given his experience and knowledge, Spike immediately understood the value of TrueSRM. What then followed the meeting was first a very personal thank you note from Spike to Laura, copying Thomas and Tracey. Then, Spike insisted on having Laura being present in all the meetings he would have with Tracey and every time they met different aspects of SRM were discussed. Finally, Spike reached out to Thomas with what he called a grand bargain. EATing wanted to launch a new comprehensive line of organic food. It believed that Heartland, despite not having the strongest credentials in that segment, would have the muscle to pull this off in a way that would leave little room for competitors. To Laura's delight, the program would be code-named "Invest."

Characteristics of Integrate Suppliers

Together with Bail Out, Integrate has the lowest number of suppliers in the SRM framework—but these suppliers are really handpicked. For a company with 1,000 suppliers, we would expect to find a handful of suppliers in this interaction model. Some companies may not even have one of them, as this model requires highly specific interaction.

In the Integrate model (Figure 7-3), the goals of the two organizations are genuinely integrated, and they work together as equal partners. This is what distinguishes Integrate. In both the Influence and Invest models, there is strong collaboration, but the supplier and customer are not quite equals. They do not function as one entity and the relationship is not so all-embracing either. Colloquially, Integrate is a partnership with a capital "P." Although an often-overused term in business, the true partnership is rare, being based on a multiyear, differentiated, and comprehensive relationship between you and your supplier to build an ecosystem that shapes the market. The supplier chosen for this model should be in your sweet spot: Its performance is flawless, and it holds the key to making you a formidable competitor by creating opportunities to grow revenues and profits while jointly shaping or reshaping the industry. You and the supplier will act very much like a single entity.

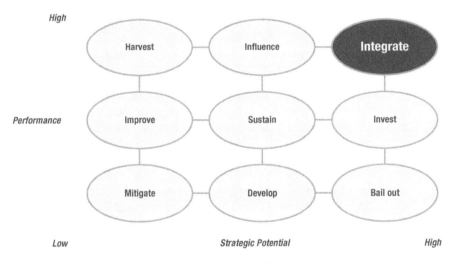

Figure 7-3. Integrate suppliers on the strategy/performance axes

It is, then, a very closely integrated relationship you build with suppliers, like a virtually integrated enterprise. Indeed, it is sometimes likened to a marriage in that it is a long-term, highly integrated relationship. In this integration, you would create a winning ecosystem to jointly shape the market.

To build and maintain such an involved relationship as the Integrate model requires substantial investment by both parties. Understand that the supplier that commits to this model takes on significant risk. By giving you highly preferential treatment, it could be limiting its own growth potential. Likewise, such concentrated, powerful Integrate relationships suggest that you should have no more than a handful of these suppliers on board.

What Kind of Behavior to Drive

There is only one right way to treat your Integrate supplier, and that is the same way you would treat your own factory. You pay it the highest respect, as it is key to making you successful. The preferred behavior of the supplier is to see the relationship as one ecosystem, or as an extension of its own company. Depending on each party's capabilities, you want to define the roles to capitalize on strengths. The supplier should be involved in making product decisions, for example deciding which market segments to attack, determining the right product or service to offer and its target cost, how to design and manufacture the product or deliver the service, and so on. It needs to think of you not only as its most desired customer, but even more as a partner in crime. If a product or service fails, you will both pay the price for it. Your success will make the supplier successful. Encourage the supplier to be proactive and come up with proposals. Provide it the platform for their ideas to be listened to and dedicate resources to drive execution.

How to Work with Integrate Suppliers

A successful Integrate relationship thrives on a shared vision and willingness to act as one smoothly running, extended enterprise. Set the stage for this by driving consistency across your own divisions, functions, and hierarchies in terms of meeting needs, budgets, and timelines with this supplier. This model makes sense only if both parties benefit in terms of profit, revenue, and growth, which means they both should be mindful of market shifts and how they may affect the other. For example, should a supplier's competitor offer the same product at a lower price, work with your Integrate supplier to meet this price by trimming specifications or improving productivity. Continually look for mutual cost reduction opportunities as well. When both parties understand each other's core competencies, they can avoid duplications and start acting as a single entity.

Note With Integrate suppliers, you meet challenges and exploit opportunities together in all regards. If a product fails in the marketplace for any reason, both should feel the pain and work together on a solution. To do this, you must understand each other's core competencies and what each of you brings to the ecosystem that you have jointly orchestrated.

The integration makes sense only if both parties benefit in terms of profit, revenue, and growth, which means that both should be mindful of market shifts and how they may affect the other. You need to be able and willing to provide meaningful volume to the supplier and, in return, increase overall significance to its business.

Governance

Getting back to building a highly integrated relationship with one of your suppliers, commitment can be demonstrated by defining a mission statement that declares the scope and purpose of a winning ecosystem. To make this relationship work, an executive sponsor is needed on both sides—chosen not based on hierarchy level but rather on their ability to drive alignment across functions, business, and hierarchies.

The effort will focus on jointly managing selected portfolio segments or even the whole portfolio, as we have observed in some cases. Manage the relationship very closely. Do not shy away from putting your A-team behind it and encourage your supplier to do the same. Encourage very close collaboration and, if needed, colocate joint teams close to decision makers. Schedule regular review meetings with management and executive sponsors, and foster a candid exchange of dialogue to eliminate any roadblocks to success. Typically, we would expect these to be needed on a frequent basis, depending on the speed of the industry. Weekly, monthly, or quarterly would be appropriate.

Case Example #1

Let's look at an example from the beverage industry: energy drinks. This was a relatively new market in the 1980s, when there were two product streams: one focused on endurance athletes who needed to hydrate their bodies and provide a sufficient level of electrolytes during high-effort sports, such as cycling. A new use and target group then emerged in the late 1980s: nightclub goers who used energy drinks as a way to stay awake and alert throughout the craze of the night. The success of the latter was driven by a company that had all of its production and supply chain outsourced to one single company. That company was Red Bull and its then partner that remains today was Rauch. In the 1980s, Rauch, a maker of fruit juices that was founded after World War I, put its belief in a single-person company—Dietrich Mateschitz with Red Bull—creating a great marketing plan and becoming its sole bottler. In return, Red Bull agreed not to work with any other bottling company. Such a commitment was risky for both parties, but Red Bull's product strength and Rauch's distribution capabilities in 90 countries made for a powerful integrated approach across the two businesses.

Today, almost 30 years later, Red Bull enjoys the largest worldwide market share in its category, selling in over 160 countries. Nevertheless, the company has remained true to its mission, and it doesn't own a single factory or truck to deliver its distinctive cans to the stores. The bottler Rauch has remained the sole supplier and still does not work for any other energy drink company. Almost half of the worldwide product is mixed and filled in two production locations in Europe.

So, what were the success factors of such a deep partnership and virtually integrated company? In the industry, there is an urban legend suggesting that this type of relationship is governed only by a handshake between both founders. While this would no doubt prove untrue for an enterprise of this magnitude—you can't seriously expect to manage business without any legal contracts—in the case of these two companies the contract itself consisted of several pages and has been left in the drawer for several years. The two businesses are so well aligned with each other, understanding each other's objectives and sharing key data, that they are seamlessly integrated. Having experienced hypergrowth in the second decade of the company, both partners had to review their combined ecosystem to allow for worldwide expansion. They considered the option of expanding and opening overseas operations, but in the end the close proximity of the Alps to pristine water and an extremely well-oiled system won. No other supplier, even some of the much larger bottlers with a much stronger presence across the world, could match what this partnership has built in the first ten years of its symbiotic existence.

Building on the success it had with Rauch, Red Bull is driving a model of very tight collaboration and building ecosystems with other key suppliers in its supply chain. The cans are still made by one main supplier that recently announced it would build a new factory literally wall-to-wall with the bottler's factory to create a highly agile supply chain. The distribution is similarly managed by a single logistics group delivering the product all over the world.

So, with its size and financial muscle, why did Red Bull not buy Rauch and its other key suppliers? The answer lies in company culture and economies of scale. The energy drink is still a relatively small market for bottled drinks. Rauch remains one of the major regional juice makers, thus giving it large economies of scale as compared to if it were only present in the Red Bull energy drink business. Same goes for all its other suppliers. Red Bull, on the other hand, is a company very focused on its young, fresh, and sporty company culture and embracing marketing and advertising as its core competence. Mixing this with operations would require making sacrifices, and over time the culture would change.

The ecosystem that has been created in the partnership allows each organization to focus on its core competence and the value it brings to the overall "system." This is advantageous vs. a full merger of the companies concerned, which would introduce greater internal managerial complexity.

"Worst Advertising" Label Rankles Heartland

In order to keep on top of things at Heartland, Thomas had developed the habit of maintaining a dashboard. It was just one sheet of paper on which he scored the different business units and functions across two dimensions—performance vs. plan. He overlaid this with his very personal gut feeling about the state of affairs. He had borrowed this approach from Autowerke's chairman and had found it highly effective. Over the past months, Heartland's soft drink division had persistently scored poorly across two dimensions. While the stagnating sales figures were a disappointment in themselves, Thomas worried most about the details behind the figures.

While Heartland's iconic soda drinks still fared quite well globally, there was a worrying trend in North America. The age group of people between 15 and 25 were abandoning Heartland products in droves and instead favoring imported energy drinks. Heartland's attempts to create its own brand of energy drinks had led to dismal results. Thomas was especially disappointed with the performance of his marketing team. After going through three agencies in two years, all they had to show was two *Consumerist* Worst Advertising Awards and horrific budget overruns.

Thomas knew that making soft drinks would do miracles for Heartland's stock market performance and decided to take matters into his own hands going forward. From his days at Autowerke, he had excellent contacts at Greenway Electronics, one of the world's biggest electronics device makers, which had taken over the smart phone market with its signature products. It took Thomas less than 15 minutes to have Tony Birch, Greenway's legendary head of industrial design, on the phone. After exchanging pleasantries and praising Greenway's latest smart phone, Thomas went directly to the topic: "Tony, I need your advice. We're losing ground in soft drinks and somehow our people don't get it. We behave like a sleepy giant, while our energy drink competitors are running circles around us. And our advertising campaigns are making matters worse, to be honest."

"Yeah, winning the Worst Advertising Award twice in a row is quite something," chuckled Tony.

"Exactly. And it is not for lack of money. We have poured a fortune into this. I believe we need an entirely different approach, and honestly speaking I don't see how we can do this from our big corporate headquarters in Fort Wayne. We seem to be completely out of touch with how young people in this country live, think, and feel. You guys at Greenway have demonstrated many times that you are capable of reinventing yourselves. You are setting trends that the entire world is following. How can we replicate this at Heartland?"

"Thomas, if someone knew how to transfer Greenland's magic formula to other companies, that guy would make a fortune writing books about it," Tony sympathized. "Even I, being at the heart of it, can't really explain it. But I might know someone who could help you. Here at Greenway we do a lot of creative things in-house, but we also work with some outside firms. There is this really creative outfit further up the valley. What they are doing is a bit hard to describe. It is somewhere between an industrial design house, a consultancy, and an advertising agency. They do really crazy stuff for us that I can't even talk about, but I believe they are what you are looking for."

Two months later, Product Maniacs, the firm Tony had recommended, was making a pitch to Thomas and his executive team. The company had requested to meet the team at 5 a.m., a highly unusual time, but had been unwilling to explain its motives. While two of the product maniacs were outlining how they would cooperate with Heartland in bringing them to the top of the mind of young consumers in America and elsewhere, Wim Kock, the founder, seemed to be somewhat absent glancing at his smart phone. Just as doubts were forming in Thomas's mind as to whether following Tony's advice was such a smart thing after all, Wim suddenly jumped to his feet and took the notebook from which they were presenting. "Gentlemen and ladies, here is the reason why we asked for a meeting so early in the day," he said with a clear South African twang in his voice. The screen flicked to a live feed from what appeared to be a rocket launch pad.

"What you see here is the launch of a supply mission to the International Space Station by a private space transport company. I happen to know the owner and got the third stage of the rocket painted like one of your energy drink cans. So while your competition is spending millions to get to the edge of space with a balloon, we can get you into orbit for free." In the background, the rocket lifted off the launchpad with the colors of the Heartland energy drink clearly visible. The powerful sound system in the conference room made the walls shake from the roar of the engines.

The video of the transport ship's liftoff and its arrival at the station, with the Heartland logo in plain view, quickly went viral on the Web. As a consequence, Heartland's energy drink sold out in most of the United States for weeks to follow. The impressive feat by Product Maniacs made the negotiations to strike a deal with Heartland a mere formality. From now on, Product Maniacs would run all product management and marketing for the energy drinks and Heartland would focus on the production and supply chain management.

Nourishing the Critical Cluster

In this chapter, we have described the three interaction models where companies will likely find fewest of their suppliers. But they are where you should place your bets if you want to make a difference by managing supplier relationships. The trick is to dedicate the right people to the job of providing the cross-functional expertise required to develop game-changing products and redefine your industry in such a way that you obtain significant competitive advantage.

We finished with the Critical Cluster to illustrate the uniqueness, intensity, and diversity of suppliers in this grouping. Far too often, companies jump to conclusions and nominate too many suppliers as Influence and Integrate candidates. In this cluster, however, the key to success is just to focus on a few critical suppliers who really matter. And this means to start off by deprioritizing many suppliers.

Putting Supplier Interaction Models to Work

Start Reaping Benefits

Now that we have introduced the overall SRM framework and the nine supplier interaction models, it is time to discuss how to make it happen. Accordingly, in this chapter we discuss a number of themes.

First, we outline the dynamic nature of SRM. The TrueSRM framework is not static. Suppliers can change position over time. We outline how this can be used to your advantage in order to give suppliers aspirational messages. This links to the concept of primary and secondary models— where the secondary model is the position that the supplier could reach or fall back to depending on performance.

We then go on to discuss the key operating-model elements that are needed to bring SRM to life. This includes the need for top-down decision making to determine strategic potential and for bottom-up input to evaluate performance. Governance models then need to be differentiated by interaction model, and resources need to be allocated to different suppliers according to their positioning.

Following this, we step back to consider the changes that take place once SRM is implemented and how success needs to be measured. In this respect, we favor a focus on competitive advantage rather than micromeasurement of benefits, which one often sees when implementing category-sourcing strategies. In fact, we see SRM as very distinct from category sourcing, and we therefore devote some time to dispelling some common confusion as to the difference between these approaches.

Having discussed these points, we then go on to talk about how to get started and then how to make SRM sustainable once you have begun. We also catch up with how our friends at Heartland are getting on with SRM implementation and consider the key factors that have driven their success.

A Dynamic Framework

The performance of suppliers varies over time, so a supplier's vertical positioning in the framework will vary as well. Also, the strategic potential of a supplier can change. Let's look at moves between interaction models in more detail.

Onboarding New Suppliers

Suppliers that are new to a company have no performance history. Typically, when onboarding new suppliers, companies apply good judgment and treat them with extra caution. Often this is sufficient to ensure a smooth onboarding without too many operational issues. Yet even so, serious shortcomings shown by new suppliers sometimes escape management's attention and lead to undesirable consequences. These include delivery shortages or quality problems. Our recommendation is to initially put all new suppliers with limited strategic potential into the Mitigate category until they have proven that their performance meets the expected level. If a new supplier in that category shows issues, it should be phased out without hesitation.

If you identify a promising new supplier that could make a difference, place it in the Develop category and dedicate company resources to bring it up to speed as quickly as possible.

For the rare diamond in the rough that is found occasionally, we recommend you go into Bail Out mode from day one. This is clearly a valuable relationship that you do not want to ruin by avoidable performance issues.

The Bail Out mode will enable you to get through these challenges and ensure that the company gains the projected competitive benefit from working with this supplier.

Supplier Moves You Are Driving

Not every model in the framework has a logical path to a neighboring model. Upward moves are perfectly possible and always desired. Suppliers can improve their performance with or without the company's support, performance you can recognize in the regular performance reviews.

The horizontal position in the framework is nearly locked in by the particularities of the supplier's business. Moves to the right require the supplier to significantly change its nature. The only possible move in this direction that we expect to see leads from Influence to Integrate. Think about a supplier who defines an industry standard. If that supplier is ready to provide products and services that allow you to achieve a sustainable competitive advantage, we would place it in the Integrate box. We are seeing elements of this behavior in several industries.

In addition to the vertical and horizontal moves, there is one possible diagonal move. If a high-strategic-potential supplier falls into a Bail Out situation, you have two options: Either you improve its performance so that it justifies its high potential or you aim to make the supplier less critical. Creating a viable alternative by qualifying another supplier to take over a portion of the volume share would move this supplier to the Sustain model. In that position, the supplier will be given the opportunity to recover its standing.

Finally, there is one move leading from Mitigate out of the framework altogether. This is because you are terminating business with that supplier unless and until there is a compelling reason to work with it again.

All of these supplier moves are illustrated in Figure 8-1.

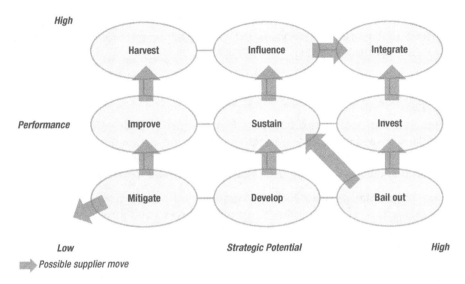

Figure 8-1. Movement within the supplier relationship model

Primary and Secondary Interaction Models

The notion that the TrueSRM framework is not static extends to the question of whether or not a supplier can fall into more than one interaction model at any point in time. Generally speaking, the idea of the SRM framework is to map the supplier as one entity and not break the mapping down to a category level.

While this is the rule, when communicating the framework and the positioning to suppliers, you should aim to send aspirational messages. Compare this to the annual feedback discussion you have with an employee. In this discussion, you would not tell the employee that she is locked into her current role and that the next level is out of reach. In order to allow for aspirational messages, we therefore introduced primary and secondary interaction models.

Following the logic of the moves introduced above, the aspirational messages should generally trend upward. For example, a supplier in Improve that is doing really well across several categories could receive the following message:

> You know, we are really quite happy with your performance lately. Across categories A, B, and C you are actually best in class. We specifically like your proposal to become your launch customer for the new product technology in category A. In our

SRM framework, we have now added Influence as secondary interaction model to Sustain. In order to get you into Influence for good, you would need to fix the delivery issues with the mainstream categories D and E.

Obviously, the secondary interaction model also can be used to send messages in the opposite direction when your happiness with a supplier is decreasing:

We have had you in Integrate for several years now. Our partnership has yielded several game-changing products and we have always appreciated your willingness to build a winning ecosystem with us. However, over the past months we have gotten increasingly concerned about a change of attitude that might be best summarized as complacency. You have let too many deadlines slip and the product quality was not always what we had expected. We want you to get more focused again, and in order to emphasize this message, we are adding the secondary interaction model Invest to our relationship.

Let us now take a look at who is preparing and delivering these messages.

Overarching SRM Decision Making

No, we don't want to introduce another administrative body. We firmly believe that corporate cultures are already overburdened with committees of all kinds. What we intend to do is to take existing cross-functional decision-making bodies and use them for SRM purposes.

In essence, SRM requires two types of decision making at the corporate level. One is bottom-up decision making regarding the evaluation of supplier performance. Another is top-down decision making that determines the strategic potential.

For evaluating performance, most companies will have cross-functional teams in place. The challenge is that they act in isolation while SRM needs a comprehensive perspective. In Chapter 5, we discussed segmentation criteria and forced ranking in detail. Here, we want to limit the discussion to who is actually making these slotting decisions. We recommend having as much of a big-picture view as possible. So, if at all feasible, the company should force-rank all of its suppliers. This will work for companies that have relatively homogeneous lines of business. For those companies, cross-functional teams should spotlight the exceptions to their leaders, meaning the really-outstanding and really-poor-performing suppliers. The leaders should then get together to assess these exceptions. With this approach, 90 percent of suppliers will fall in the middle category and debate will be limited to 10 percent of suppliers, normally a doable task.

For companies with a diverse set of businesses—think ThyssenKrupp with steel mills, shipyards, engineering services, automotive suppliers, and elevator makers—force ranking all suppliers will not make sense. For these types of conglomerates, we recommend applying performance ranking at the level of each individual line of business, or for each distinct subsidiary.

Determining the strategic potential of a supplier should be done top down by the cross-functional leadership team. Once a year, the leaders get together and decide which of the suppliers have a medium or a high strategic potential. Again, we assume that less than 10 percent of suppliers will fall into these two categories and therefore that the task will be perfectly manageable.

Note   When determining the strategic potential of your suppliers, remember that in most cases only 10 percent of them will be in a position to help you gain competitive advantages.

Governance Models by Supplier

For suppliers in the Harvest, Improve, and Sustain categories, not much will change. You will continue measuring their performance periodically and provide feedback. While their positioning in the framework will not be a secret, you will not proactively communicate it. Other than working to improve their performance, there is not much the suppliers can do to change their positioning.

Suppliers that fall into the Mitigate, Develop, and Bail Out interaction models will not be engaged in a broader discussion of their relationship. Time is often critical and matters are urgent, so specific business needs to improve performance or address failings will dominate the agenda.

Where things will change significantly is in the Influence, Integrate, and Invest interaction models. You will proactively inform suppliers in these categories as to where they stand, develop clear roadmaps and account plans, and drive aligned agendas through joint steering committees. In particular:

- For Influence suppliers, you will focus on formalizing the process to bring into sync your respective product, technology, and service roadmaps. In order to make this happen, a cross-functional steering group will not only ensure smooth communication with the supplier but also establish consistency across Procurement, Engineering, and Product Marketing. With this fine-tuned approach, you will be able to win where it matters.

- Invest suppliers will initially receive a lot of feedback from you. What used to be isolated performance reports will be condensed into a thoroughly researched performance gap analysis. This analysis will be shared with the supplier's senior executives, together with clear performance targets. You will assign program managers to drive improvement and dedicate substantial executive attention to guiding the supplier in the right direction.

- Working with Integrate suppliers will be the masterpiece of your SRM efforts. First, you will develop a mission statement together with the supplier, specifying what it is that you want to achieve jointly. Then, you will define a step-by-step roadmap that describes how the supplier can earn the right to exclusively "own" a product market segment. A binding incentive mechanism will ensure that your objectives and those of the supplier are fully aligned, and that both parties act as partners with an entrepreneurial spirit. Finally, a joint executive leadership team will oversee the product market segments in scope from a holistic, end-to-end perspective.

Roles in SRM

As we have seen, each of the nine supplier interaction models has its specific governance structure. There are several common denominators, though, that are relevant across the entire SRM framework.

First and foremost, the old principle of presenting one face to the supplier should be followed. We know it is easier said than done, but if suppliers are able to put a key account manager in place, customers should certainly be able to appoint one relationship owner as well.

Tip The supplier should, ideally, deal with one customer point person. Whom you choose, however, is critical.

The position of the supplier in the SRM framework will largely determine the seniority and functional affiliation of the relationship owner—the primary "go to" person who is responsible for managing the relationship with the supplier. For suppliers that are in Harvest, Improve, and Mitigate, the relationship owner will most likely come from Procurement. Given the low strategic potential, involvement from other functions will be limited. The seniority level of the relationship owner will correlate with the spending that is attributed to that supplier.

Who Is the Best Relationship Owner?

For suppliers in Develop, an engineering or manufacturing representative might be appointed as relationship owner. Typically, these functions have the strongest vested interest in bringing this promising new supplier up to speed and making it ready to bring new products and services to the market.

For suppliers in Sustain, the relationship owner will probably come from the function that has the highest level of interaction with that supplier. If, for example, you are dealing with a marketing-and-advertising firm, it would come naturally for a senior marketing executive to own the relationship.

Moving on to Influence, the choice will vary by industry. If it is about a supplier that defines an industry standard, the relationship might even be owned by the CEO. This will, for example, be the case for an airline, where the chief executive will own the relationship to Boeing and Airbus.

In Integrate, owning the relationship will be highly time-consuming given the complexity of the relationship and the associated cognitive load. It is unlikely that a candidate at the top executive level can be freed up from other duties to attend to the required extent; therefore, the relationship owner will probably be a mid-ranking executive who is highly respected internally and passionate about building a game-changing ecosystem.

For Invest suppliers, the relationship owner will mostly guide the supplier in comprehensive programs to build capabilities. Given the nature of this task, the relationship owner will most likely have a technical background.

Bail Out suppliers follow their own rules. As the Bail Out will be governed by a task force or tiger team, the leader of this team will take over the ownership of the relationship from the regular relationship owner for the duration of the bailout.

Maintaining Consistency in Your Message

Once the consistency in the communication channel is established, you need to ensure consistency in content. Today, most companies do have supplier evaluation processes established. Regardless of whether they are as structured as we suggest in Chapter 5 or not, sending confusing messages to suppliers is a common pitfall. We have seen quarterly supplier evaluations fluctuate so wildly that even the most well-meaning supplier will not be able to make any sense of the feedback it receives.

As a fix, we suggest making the supplier evaluation simple and focusing it on a few key criteria that really matter. Also, the cross-functional team that produces these evaluations should be characterized by continuity. The relationship owner should have the final say in the rating and feedback the supplier receives.

Employing Account Plans

With consistency in communication and content established, the cross-functional team needs to align on where to drive the supplier. Account plans have been found useful in this context. The account plan describes at a high level where the relationship with the supplier should be heading mid- to long-term. Once this account plan has been agreed upon by internal stakeholders, it is usually shared with the supplier. It is good for the supplier to understand what its customer's intention is and what it could get out of the relationship if this intention is fulfilled.

Meetings with Suppliers

This leaves the final communication topic of regular meetings with suppliers. Suppliers in Harvest, Improve, and Mitigate do not require large formal meetings, and can be dealt with more on an ad hoc basis, such as when the sales representative happens to make his usual call.

For all other suppliers, you should provide a great deal of attention to the preparation and execution of meetings. We have seen quarterly meetings deteriorate into a ritual that can be best compared to going to mass on Sunday. The representative for the supplier comes to the sermon and listens, confesses the company's sins, promises to do better in the future, walks out, and continues with business as usual. This is a massive missed opportunity. It takes a great deal of effort and money to get key stakeholders from both parties into one room. As a general rule, the relationship owners from both sides should agree on the key topics to be covered in the sequence of meetings over the next year or so, based on the account plan. Then, the functional teams from both sides should be tasked with preparing meaningful status reports and outlooks with regard to the progress vs. the account plan. Bringing this more forward-looking mindset into meetings with suppliers adds a lot of value to the relationship.

Where to Put Resources

As already hinted at in the previous paragraph, our SRM framework will lead to a quite substantial reallocation of resources. Among other things, our aim is to help companies to put their resources where it really matters. Today, in most companies the available resources are spread relatively evenly across suppliers.

We are suggesting a highly asymmetric allocation, starting with managing at arm's length the vast majority of suppliers that reside in Improve and Harvest. Managing these suppliers can tie up a lot of resources, but if you are brutally honest, you will see there is little to gain by spending as much time and effort as you do. This is why we recommend having relatively junior procurement people own the relationships with these suppliers.

Suppliers in Mitigate can still be managed by relatively junior procurement people but will require more of a time commitment. This is why we recommend making decisions swiftly. Having a supplier hanging in this interaction model for more than a couple of months would definitely be wrong.

Note   Suppliers shouldn't reside in the Mitigate category for more than a couple of months. By that point, if you have done your job properly, they should be moved up or out.

The heavy resource allocation should be at the opposite end of the SRM framework—in Integrate, Invest, and, if needed, in Bail Out. With Integrate suppliers, you should aspire to build a winning ecosystem that will allow game-changing moves. It is evident that these relationships should be prioritized over all others and have the first call on any available resource. This is where the company will win or lose ultimately.

For suppliers in Invest, the resource allocation should be more cautious. After all, we believe these suppliers could become great partners but we still need the proof of concept. Therefore, the emphasis in Invest is to guide the investments of the supplier in terms of funds and talent allocation without committing too many of the own resources.

Bailouts will drain substantial resources when they occur. But there is little we can do about this. Our recommendation is to front-load bailouts by sending people to be there (physically) without hesitation. The old proverb "Better being safe than sorry" still applies and we have seen that too many companies hesitate in the critical early days of a bailout. These highly nonstandard situations cannot be solved via e-mail and phone calls; having boots on the ground early makes a big difference.

Suppliers in the middle three interaction models should receive resources but with caution. For suppliers in Influence, the key question is, "Can they be influenced?" If the supplier is ready to engage in collaborations that lead to a tangible competitive advantage, committing resources makes perfect sense. But all of us have seen the skillful efforts of suppliers that define an industry standard that only maintain the status quo. Accepting invitations to conferences, dinners, and golf courses can be a useful way to build a rapport of trust and mutual understanding. But these things have to provide a yield. If nothing tangible has surfaced after a year, it should become clear that the supplier does not want to engage under the terms of this interaction model. After this realization, it seems appropriate to sit down with the supplier and explain that you are scaling back the relationship to Sustain.

In Sustain, the resource requirement should be minimal. Efforts should be limited to reminding the supplier of the growth potential that would open up if it improved its performance.

Suppliers in Develop will receive quite a lot of support and resources. One way to justify this commitment is to have the supplier pay for it. A best-practice example from the automotive industry is to establish supplier development teams that act like external consultants. These teams have daily rates that get charged to the suppliers, who are encouraged to use these services. A positive side effect of this practice is that a supplier will take services it has to pay for more seriously.

What Changes for Suppliers

With the SRM framework in place, everything changes for suppliers. Imagine your company having one common language to define supplier relationships, alignment across functions, alignment across lines of business, and alignment across hierarchy levels! In this scenario, we will see winners and losers among suppliers.

Those suppliers that so far have dedicated most of their time to playing games, to finding the weak link in your organization will lose under these new terms. Their scheming and politicking will be brought to unforgiving daylight and they will have little time to adjust.

The winners will be suppliers that always had good intentions but were frustrated by conflicting messages and lack of clear direction. They will finally find a framework they can plug into and find their spot to best add value.

HOW TO MEASURE THE SUCCESS OF SRM

SRM cannot be measured in terms of cost savings. This is what category-sourcing strategies are about. At the highest level, the success of SRM can be measured by the incremental competitive advantage that can be attributed to suppliers. Competitive advantage will mean different things to different companies, but it can manifest itself as follows:

- Successful product and service innovations that have been brought to market and helped the company gain market share

- A higher profit margin due to higher price levels that can be achieved in the market and those due to overall reduced cost of goods sold

- Higher availability rates and shorter delivery lead times

- Better product and service quality, better and easier service, and happier customers

How SRM Relates to Category-Sourcing Strategies

In the process of developing the SRM framework, we have noticed wide-ranging confusion about the distinction between SRM and category strategies. In some literature, SRM is even defined as the implementation stage of a category strategy.

For the following comparison of SRM and category strategies, we are referring to the Purchasing Chessboard as the standard framework for developing category strategies.

As discussed in earlier chapters, the Purchasing Chessboard was developed by A. T. Kearney consultants in 2008 and has since been applied by thousands of companies across all industries and continents. The idea behind the Purchasing Chessboard is that category-sourcing strategies should be based upon considerations around demand power and supply power.

A company has a high demand power if its spending for a certain category represents a significant portion of the overall supply industry revenue in that sector. Additional factors that increase demand power are the opportunities for innovations that suppliers can draw from working with the company and the image boost a supplier would get from having the company on its reference list.

Similarly, a supplier has a high supply power if its revenue within a certain category represents a significant portion of the overall supply industry revenue in that sector. Additional factors that increase supply power are the ability of the supplier to drive innovation for the category and to create a pull with the company's customers (think of "Intel inside"). Suppliers that own critical patents and are monopolists in a certain sector enjoy the highest supply power.

The Purchasing Chessboard is defined by two axes, demand power and supply power (Figure 8-2). At the highest level, the chessboard is segmented into four quadrants:

- *High demand power:* An example is a big carmaker (e.g., Volkswagen) that buys forged parts. There must be hundreds, if not thousands, of forged-part manufacturers throughout the world, and out of those there must be at least several dozen that are qualified to meet Volkswagen's quality and volume requirements. In this case, Volkswagen is a buyer in a position of overwhelming power vis-à-vis its forgings suppliers, and it is able to exploit competition among its suppliers to its own advantage.

- *High supply and demand power:* If Volkswagen now wishes to buy engine management systems from Bosch, the situation is completely different. In many segments, Bosch holds a de facto monopoly. Nevertheless, Bosch is just as dependent on the big carmakers as they are on Bosch. In this case, securing joint, long-term advantages is unquestionably in the interest of both parties.

- *High supply power:* Even the demand power of a big carmaker has its limits, especially when oligopolistic market conditions prevail. A good example is the purchasing of traded commodities, such as platinum for catalysts. While Volkswagen certainly purchases a large quantity of platinum, it is fully dependent upon the quoted prices of metal exchanges. Companies confronted by high supply power will consistently strive to bring about fundamental change in the nature of the demand in order to free themselves from the control of the supplier.

- *Low supply and demand power:* An example of low demand power on the part of a big carmaker is air travel. The situation is more balanced than in the preceding example, however, since deregulation of the airline market has actually produced results. Along with negotiating discounts, a key question to ask in this context is whether traveling by plane is necessary or whether it could be avoided altogether. Thus, the company is largely able to steer its own demand.

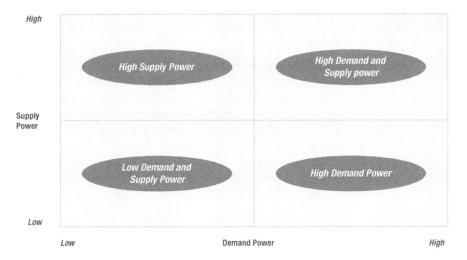

Figure 8-2. The Purchasing Chessboard: 4 Basic Strategies

The four quadrants of the Purchasing Chessboard also represent its four basic strategies—leveraging competition among suppliers, seeking joint advantage with suppliers, changing the rules of the game, and managing spend. These are shown in Figure 8-2.

The most detailed version of the Purchasing Chessboard is comprised of 64 detailed methods—16 associated with each basic strategy. This is the one typically in use by procurement executives who are developing category strategies with their teams. The detailed version of the Purchasing Chessboard is shown in Figure 8-3.[1]

---

[1] For more information about the Purchasing Chessboard, please refer to www.purchasingchessboard.com.

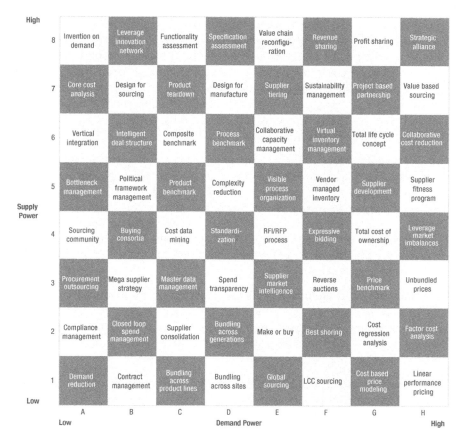

Figure 8-3. The Purchasing Chessboard: 64 Detailed Methods

In our view, SRM and the Purchasing Chessboard cover very different areas and have quite different objectives. While SRM is about leveraging a company's size and driving desired supplier behavior, the Purchasing Chessboard is about developing the right category strategies. As outlined in the previous paragraph, success is measured by very different key performance indicators as well. The success of SRM is measured by competitive advantage achieved and defined very broadly. The success of the application of the Purchasing Chessboard is predominantly measured by cost reductions achieved with suppliers. At a secondary level, the Purchasing Chessboard also aims at creating value with suppliers, but this value creation is always strictly linked to a given category.

Let's now examine if there is a correlation between the SRM framework and the Purchasing Chessboard.

Suppliers in Harvest, Improve, and Mitigate have low strategic potential with categories that can fall almost anywhere on the Purchasing Chessboard. The only area on the chessboard that will be mostly untapped by categories provided by these suppliers is the upper-right quadrant representing the "Seek joint advantage with suppliers" basic strategy. The reason for this is that high supply power and high demand power in the upper-right-hand side quadrant of the chessboard would translate into medium or even high strategic potential.

Suppliers that fall into Influence, Sustain, Develop, Integrate, Invest, and Bail Out in the SRM framework have medium or high strategic potential with categories that can fall almost anywhere on the Purchasing Chessboard. The only other area of the purchasing that will be mostly untapped by categories provided by these suppliers is the lower-left-hand-side quadrant, representing the "Manage spend" basic strategy. The reason for this is that low supply power and low demand power in this quadrant translate into low strategic potential.

For suppliers that fall into Bail Out, the category or product that causes the bailout will almost certainly sit in the upper half of the chessboard. This category or product will involve a novel technology that this supplier has been one of the very few players on the planet to master. The supplier therefore enjoys high supply power for this product.

With these considerations in mind, we can summarize that at a high level, the SRM framework and the Purchasing Chessboard are mutually independent tools. The only exception is the Strategic Potential axis in the SRM framework, which is weakly correlated with the Purchasing Chessboard in the following ways:

- Low Strategic Potential in the SRM framework excludes the combination of high supply power and high demand power in the Purchasing Chessboard.

- Medium and high Strategic Potential in the SRM framework exclude the combination of low supply power and low demand power in the Purchasing Chessboard.

How to Get Started

The SRM framework in this book is structured, repeatable, and scalable. Putting it to work is more of a change-management effort than an intellectual challenge. In our experience, suppliers appreciate the introduction of the framework, but internal resistance should be expected.

Note Expect resistance to the SRM framework internally. As always, it's easier to maintain the status quo. To attain meaningful change, top executives must endorse the initiative and see the change through.

Resistance will first build against one of the key objectives of SRM— leveraging the company's size. Realizing this objective will require coordination across functions, lines of business, and hierarchy levels. Out of routine, for all involved players, it will be easier to do what they have done in the past and go out to engage with the supplier without coordinating upfront. Change here will not come without strong endorsement from the very top of the organization. We recommend using a very simple line to convince the CEO to lend his or her endorsement. The best argument is to equate suppliers with customers. Everyone usually understands readily that internal alignment and consistent messages are needed when dealing with customers. The use of key account management and CRM (Customer Relationship Management) is well-established on the "sell" side. The same disciplines are consequently needed on the "buy side," namely, SRM.

Resistance will also be strong when the initial segmentation of suppliers takes place. Too many owners of supplier relationships will want to see "their" suppliers in the top-right-hand corner of the SRM framework. We cautioned against the inflationary use of the term *partner* in the introduction of this book. And we agree that it is a nicer job to inform a supplier that it resides in Integrate than to explain why Sustain or Harvest are more appropriate. The following steps have worked well for avoiding resistance to the results of the segmentation:

- Compare team members' segmentation to their annual performance evaluations. No organization would tolerate having all employees in the top category. This would make the evaluation process meaningless and demotivate top performers. The same is true in SRM.

- Refrain from overcommunicating the segmentation results. Suppliers with low strategic potential—that is, those in Harvest, Improve, and Mitigate—do not need to be informed about the SRM framework and their positioning at all. We are talking about 90 percent of suppliers here and with this measure, the workload associated with getting SRM going is reduced as well. There is also no need for keeping SRM a secret, though, and all interested suppliers will eventually learn about it. But for those 90 percent, the time when they actively ask is an early-enough point at which to inform them.

- Work with primary and secondary interaction models. As previously explained, the primary interaction model indicates where the supplier really sits today, but the secondary interaction model can be used to deliver a more aspirational message.

The most resistance can be expected when a supplier is entering the Integrate interaction model. Let's discuss this by looking at a case example.

Case Example

A major carmaker with several brands had a colorful relationship history with its largest supplier of interior systems. Interior systems encompassed everything that the passengers in the car could see, touch, smell, and hear. Many executives at the carmaker agreed that the supplier had played a crucial role in making several car lines very successful in the market, but there had also been ups and downs in the relationship.

What counted for the carmaker was to achieve a high market share at a competitive cost. Since the interior system accounted for a significant portion of the externally sourced expenditure of a car, the supplier was the key focus of several past cost-reduction initiatives. The supplier got sourced many times and now claimed to be in the red with several product lines. The carmaker did not believe this and substantial management resources were dedicated on both sides to haggle over cost.

From the perspective of the supplier, it was quite hard to do business with the carmaker. It got conflicting messages when talking to Procurement, Engineering, and Product Management. Also, the different brands of the carmaker were not aligned with regard to the supplier. The supplier could be in favor with one brand while falling out of favor with another. At the top, the CEOs of the two companies entertained a quite-active communication channel but did not align internally, which led to additional confusion, mostly to the disadvantage of the supplier.

In summary, all these factors had pushed the supplier into a reactive mindset. The supplier had sat back and waited for the carmaker to give instructions, based on which the supplier would execute. Whenever there had been a disagreement, the supplier would respond, "But you told me to do so."

At a certain point in time, key players at the carmaker recognized that there was a big missed opportunity with this supplier. With sluggish global car markets and increased competition from new competitors, there was a realization that the future of the automotive industry would be determined by a competition of ecosystems. They then defined five key success factors for the collaboration with the supplier:

1. Bringing the supplier in for the concept phase already as a partner with equal rights

2. Granting the supplier exclusivity in certain product market segments

3. Sharing responsibility for volume, price, and margin with the supplier

4. Making engineering, marketing, and procurement decisions jointly with the supplier

5. Clearly aligning competencies to avoid duplications and overlaps

First and foremost, the supplier needed to be elevated from its reactive mindset. With the supplier just executing the instructions and specifications of the carmaker, major opportunities were lost. Not only did the carmaker not leverage the vast experience and insight of the supplier into its recent developments in interior systems, but the specifications it developed often were difficult and expensive to make. Bringing the supplier in for the concept phase already as a partner with equal rights led to a true paradigm shift. Resident engineers and product planners from the supplier joined the carmaker's cross-functional product-development teams. The supplier's experts completely changed the way the carmaker was looking at interior systems. For the first time, the carmaker's key source of inspiration was not the models that competitors displayed at auto shows but the input of the supplier, which involved very concrete and feasible ideas on how the interior system of the future should really look.

For the supplier to open up so radically to the carmaker, it needed assurances that its breakthrough ideas would not just be taken from it and then realized with one of its competitors. Therefore, the carmaker granted the supplier exclusivity for those car lines for which the supplier had injected its breakthrough ideas. There also was a very explicit understanding that this exclusivity had no limits. Provided that the carmaker's volume and profitability targets for the car lines in the scope of the agreement were met, the scope would be expanded to additional car lines. In the best case, the supplier would eventually own the interior systems of all car lines. Under that agreement, it was also made clear that car lines within the scope would be out of reach for the supplier's competitors. Since it had so heavily influenced the overall design of the interior system, a competitive quote that would just cover making and assembling the parts would be considered irrelevant.

As an assurance for the carmaker that the supplier would not just lean back and relax, a set of strict incentives and penalties were agreed upon. In fact, the supplier shared the entrepreneurial risk for the car lines in scope. It took some time for the supplier to agree to this principle, but once comprehensive marketing research confirmed that the interior system was indeed a key criterion for the end customers' buying decision, the supplier agreed. In the incentive and penalty scheme, volume, price, and margin targets for the car lines were established. For every unit of positive deviation from the target, the supplier would receive a bonus payment; for every unit of negative deviation from the target, the supplier would have to pay a penalty.

In order to agree to the incentive-and-penalty scheme, the supplier requested that it have a say in all operations, marketing, and sales decisions concerning the car lines in scope. After some hesitation, the carmaker understood that there was no way to avoid doing this and opened up to the supplier. Functional task forces, staffed from both the carmaker and the supplier, were established to work on day-to-day decision making. A joint executive steering committee would now provide strategic guidance to these task forces.

Under the cost pressures of a sluggish market, both parties then looked into synergy potentials. This initiative was driven by the carmaker, which first revisited its core competencies in interior systems. Everything that was not considered noncore was by definition to be performed by the supplier. This exercise yielded head-count savings across several functions with by far the biggest chunk in engineering.

Creating Momentum for SRM

Implementing any of the five key success factors will meet a substantial level of internal resistance in any company. Bringing the supplier in as a partner with equal rights at the concept stage will frighten engineering and product-marketing people. Granting the supplier exclusivity for certain product market segments will raise concerns about losing leverage and competitiveness. Sharing responsibility for fundamental operations, sales, and marketing with a supplier will be a stretch for all involved parties. And aligning core competencies, with the resulting reduction in head counts, will clearly not be welcomed by those affected.

So, how can the required momentum to introduce SRM be created? As usual, it is the right combination of focus, quick wins, and baby steps. Focusing on those suppliers that will make a difference is the first ingredient for success. Suppliers in Influence, Integrate, and Invest are those that really warrant the attention of scarce management resources. Even in companies that have thousands of suppliers, not more than a couple of handfuls of suppliers will fall into those three interaction models. Therefore, focusing on those suppliers will ensure that resources for SRM are not spread too thin.

Delivering a couple of quick wins is paramount. If SRM enables a new technology from an Influence supplier to be used with a customer, a hot-selling product to be developed with an Integrate supplier, and a tangible performance breakthrough to be achieved with an Invest supplier, many stakeholders will want to join the bandwagon. Therefore, a lot of thought should be dedicated to what these quick wins can be even before rolling out SRM.

Finally, taking baby steps in a controlled, manageable environment is better than drowning in complexity. In the automotive interior systems example just looked at, the Integrate relationship with the supplier was initially limited to two car lines. Those car lines had a team of executives that was generally friendly and supportive to the SRM initiative. They provided an environment in which quick wins could flourish and attempts to derail the idea were deemed to be unlikely.

How to Make SRM Sustainable

In order to be sustainable, SRM must evolve from the initiative status to being embedded in the company's culture, organization, and DNA. Realistically, this will be a multiyear process with numerous setbacks and disappointments. Therefore, it is important for the company's leadership team to keep the eye on the prize. If done right, SRM will become a competitive advantage that cannot be substituted by old-school, one-size-fits-all supplier squeezing.

Heartland's TrueSRM In The News

Let's return to the story at Heartland. We are now two years on from the events of the month of mayhem that are described in Chapter 3. Thomas, Laura, and the team have successfully put SRM in place. As described in Chapter 4, the procurement function has been transformed to focus on high-value activities and supplier relationships. Heartland has systematically implemented the different interaction models across its supply base. As shown in Chapters 5, 6, and 7, the company has gained considerable benefit in the process.

Heartland's success has started to attract considerable interest in the marketplace. This has come about in several ways. First, the restructuring of the procurement function became very well-known externally. Heartland's hiring of nontraditional MBA graduates attracted considerable attention. The subsequent creation of the supplier development function also became very well-known and was seen in some quarters as unusual for the food industry. However, the reporting of these developments did not go beyond the procurement press and specialist supply-management blogs.

Another development also attracted considerable attention. This was the decision to replace the existing creative agency, Delta Creative. Of course, many companies replace suppliers. However, decisions to replace creative agencies are rarely taken lightly. This particular relationship was also of such long standing that it really did cause quite a stir. It was reported heavily in both the procurement press and throughout the marketing world.

So far, these developments did not attract attention in the general business world, nor in the mainstream business press. This all changed with the three developments that are outlined in Chapter 7. First, the appearance of the Heartland energy drink brand in orbit and the subsequent announcement of the relationship with Product Maniacs caused excitement well beyond the marketing world. Heartland had always been seen as a very conservative business. Admittedly, this was perhaps a slightly unfair estimation. The very way that Thomas had been recruited as CPO from a chance meeting with the then CEO on a plane trip is just one example that exposes the lie in this. Nevertheless, this was the way that the company was seen. The relationship with Product Maniacs really was something else. Close observers of Heartland were now starting to wonder whether something more systematic was taking place to change things.

The second was the launch of the joint organic food range in conjunction with the high-end grocery EATing. Previously, EATing had eschewed such tie-ups with suppliers. Despite being a high-end food business, it had treated its private-label suppliers as pure subcontractors. The relationship with Heartland really was something else. This was picked up by the mainstream business press in a very significant way.

The third development that really made observers feel that something systematic was taking place was the co-commercialization of the color-changing film with Caledonian. This innovation went viral in the news media and caused a 10 percent increase in Heartland's stock price.

The world was now sitting up and taking notice. Perceptive observers were now starting to make the link that the "something" that was going on was related to how Heartland was working with external suppliers. Foremost among these observers was Elisabeth Huttich, a top writer for one of the leading German-language business journals that was also syndicated in the English speaking world. Thomas's role as CEO of such a traditionally Midwestern business as Heartland had always been a great human-interest story for her readers. She had interviewed Thomas when he became CEO at Heartland. Elisabeth was probably the first external observer to deduce that Heartland was behaving "differently" toward its external supply base. She reached out to Thomas and requested an interview for an article she decided to write called "Has Heartland Found the Secret Sauce for Working with Suppliers?"

So, one chilly February morning, in Fort Wayne, Elisabeth was ushered into Thomas's office, where Thomas and Laura were there waiting for her. So was Emma Jenkins, the head of investor relations. She wanted to chaperone both Thomas and Laura to help them ensure that they were mindful of corporate codes of conduct with respect to price sensitive information.

Elisabeth and Thomas greeted each other with the traditional continental kiss on each cheek. Elisabeth had not previously met Laura and Emma. After introductions and some small talk, Elisabeth got down to business. "As I e-mailed you about, Thomas, I am really interested in understanding exactly what Heartland is doing in supplier relationship management. The success you are all having is amazing," she said. "Everyone else seems to struggle. What are you all doing?"

Thomas looked at Laura. "Laura, you have orchestrated things. Why don't you tell Elisabeth what we have been doing?" Then, he paused and looked at Elisabeth. "Laura can't tell you everything though. We don't want the whole world copying us in everything we do. We need to keep some secrets," he said with a smile.

Laura then started to explain the development of the interaction models to Elisabeth, the use of the framework to segment the supply base, and then some of the actual cases of what Heartland had done with specific suppliers. Elisabeth was clearly fascinated by Laura's storytelling. After an hour or so, they paused as coffee was brought in.

Elisabeth sat back and asked: "So, Laura, was it just about having the framework? Lots of companies have supplier segmentation frameworks, but they have not achieved the type of success you have achieved. Was there more to it?"

"Yes," answered Laura. "Having the right framework that focuses on current performance and strategic value matters. But the really key thing is that we have made it a living-and-breathing organism that is intrinsic to how we run the business. It is far more pervasive than a pure procurement approach."

"How so?"

"Well. First of all, we never lose sight of what SRM is about. You know many companies think it is about process, score cards, or is somehow an adjunct to category sourcing. "

"You do hear that," Elisabeth agreed.

"Well, it's not. It is about how you drive desired supplier behaviors. Process, score cards, and governance forums are only a means to an end. Too many organizations that we talk to see SRM in these exclusive terms. These things matter, but they must be implemented in context and be appropriate to the supplier's interaction model and the things you are seeking to achieve."

Elisabeth nodded in agreement.

"Second," Laura continued, "we do not confuse SRM with category sourcing. We use the Purchasing Chessboard to determine our strategies in category sourcing. It is all about how we choose to buy specific goods and services that happen to have the same supply markets. That is not the same thing as driving desired supplier behavior. Not at all."

Laura paused. "I see," offered Elisabeth. She thought for a couple of seconds. "Are they really so different though? Threatening to launch a bidding contest with a supplier surely has some impact on behavior? I am not sure I really agree with your point."

"Let me explain it more carefully," said Laura. "It's a bit subtle. Sure, category sourcing and SRM need to be complementary. The sourcing levers a company chooses to use have a big impact on supplier behavior. Your example of a tender is perfectly valid. Suppose we have an Integrate supplier. We have a very close relationship with the company that we gain competitive advantage from. We then decide to threaten a tender or create a contractual dispute that we bring the lawyers in over. It's bound to affect the relationship if we do these things. And, we have to think about that when we choose our sourcing levers. This does not mean we won't get aggressive if we have to, by the way, but we think about the wider impacts if we do need to. The key point remains, though, that category sourcing is about how I choose to buy goods and services and SRM is about how I drive desired supplier behavior."

"I see that," said Elisabeth.

"Third, we have made a corporate decision that SRM is the right thing to do. The success of SRM at Heartland has therefore never been measured in cost terms. Our focus has been much more holistic—on innovation, risk reduction, and revenue enhancement. We have resisted the urge to micromeasure the impact of our activities."

"That must have been quite hard to pull off," commented Elisabeth. "The need for business cases is a refrain that one constantly hears."

"We have stuck to our approach. Thomas strongly drove, and still does drive, the vision. He has given us top cover to focus on this. It's a bit like sustainability—you are, in my view, either committed to it or not. To subject every aspect of it to a micro-financial-business case is to miss the point and will ultimately be self-defeating. We have very much taken that approach to SRM."

"That is very inspiring," said Elisabeth.

"The fourth point is consistent with our strategic mindset for SRM. We have driven our approach to supplier interactions top-down from a corporation-wide perspective. Many people make the mistake of driving segmentation entirely via categories. With this approach, different parts of the business, or worse still, procurement category managers, nominate 'strategic suppliers.' The problem is that everyone wants to feel they have some strategic suppliers. So, you get suppliers that, for our business, could never lead to real innovation or competitive advantage being nominated as strategic. I have heard of facilities' suppliers being labeled as 'strategic' because they are big. For us, they are Harvest, and certainly not Integrate."

"I can see the problem," said Elisabeth.

"It stems very often from failing to distinguish between category sourcing and SRM, as we already discussed. Instead, we drive our resource allocation and the effort that we devote to particular suppliers entirely top-down from our framework. So, we devote most attention to the Critical Cluster for positive reasons and to the Problem Children for negative ones. We put far less attention into the Ordinaries."

"Is it really so special to prioritize in this way?"

"Most organizations prioritize in a much less top-down way," Laura explained. "They tend to drive resource allocation and effort from categories and size of spending rather than from a true perspective of performance and value. The resource prioritization is not just about how we allocate procurement people. We have found that the biggest benefit is how we allocate management time and decision making time. It's a mindset thing. For example, we found that one of the suppliers we now rate as Harvest had an account team of 12 people and they were involved in an executive-level meeting every couple of days. They are a good-performing supplier, but this was completely inappropriate. On the other hand, we now consciously devote far-more executive-management time to organizations such as Product Maniacs now. We have completely changed the way we think about the priority we give to different supplier relationships."

Elisabeth sensed that Laura was really very excited by what had been done. "It's a really inspiring story," she said. "I am very impressed. Is there anything else you would like to highlight? "

"Well," said Laura. "The fifth point is that we treat this as a dynamic thing. That has enabled us to focus on giving suppliers consistent, aligned, and aspirational messages. That is something we are still learning, I would say. It only comes with experience. Suppliers can change position. Performance can ebb and flow."

"Can you explain?"

"Well, let me start with performance. We do not want suppliers becoming complacent. To avoid this, we took a decision in the past year to force-rank every supplier in performance from an overall Heartland perspective, irrespective of category."

"That must have been quite a challenge."

"Indeed," said Laura, "it was. But, we stuck to it. It forced some challenging internal conversations. Initially, we got too hooked up on small differences between suppliers that were all broadly in the middle of the bell curve anyway. That was not so helpful.

Then we realized it would be much more useful to focus on understanding who the bottom 10 percent of performers were and who the top performers were. For the bottom performers, it has forced tough internal conversations on whether we should replace them. It has also meant we have been giving some of the suppliers very aspirational messages to improve. This has been particularly the case where a supplier is performing poorly but is potentially quite valuable for us. In such a case, replacing them is far less of an option. There are already encouraging signs of improvement among some of them."

Elisabeth nodded in understanding. Laura went on. "We are just about ready now to refresh the ranking work. We learned a lot the first time around. It will be more focused this time and we will be even sharper on delivering the right messages."

"What about strategic potential?" asked Elisabeth. "Is that dynamic too?"

"Much less so," Laura said. "It's much harder for strategic potential to change over time, because it is governed by the specifics of a supplier's business. But it can occasionally change as well, of course."

"How so?"

"Well, there is an example of an Influence supplier that we are reclassifying as Integrate. It is Caledonian Packaging, headquartered in Edinburgh. The level of cooperation we are achieving and the access we are now getting to its future product pipeline is really quite breathtaking. We are coming up with some great stuff together. So, that is—"

Emma, who had been largely silent up to now, interrupted. "Could you treat that as off the record, Elisabeth? I would prefer you did not publish it."

"I understand," said Elisabeth. "You have all been very open. I respect your need for confidentiality."

Laura blushed slightly. "Yes, thank you. We are not quite ready to communicate this with Caledonian yet, either. We have been hinting at the reclassification for a while."

"Yes," said Thomas. "My good friend Calum Drummond is salivating to get that designation. I want to make him sweat just a little longer before we finalize it!" They all smiled and Laura stopped blushing.

"The fact that such a respected CEO pays such attention to how you classify his business really brings home to me how powerful this is," said Elisabeth. She noticed the time and that the two hours scheduled for the session were nearly over. It felt like a natural endpoint anyway. "On that note, thank you very much for such an interesting morning."

She exchanged her goodbyes and left for the airport. That afternoon, Elisabeth boarded her flight back to Munich. As the dinner service started, she reviewed her notes and captured five key success factors for SRM that she would use in her article.

Key Factors

Let's look at the Five Key Success Factors that Elisabeth captured:

1. Never lose sight that SRM is about driving desired supplier behavior based on the appropriate interaction model. Process, governance, and score cards are purely means to support that end.

2. SRM is complementary with but distinct from category sourcing. Category sourcing is about how you buy things, not about how you drive supplier behavior.

3. Make a strategic decision to implement SRM because it is the right thing to do and will deliver competitive advantage. Resist the temptation to micromeasure benefits.

4. Drive the segmentation of suppliers and prioritization of resources across the organization. Resist the urge to segment category by category or to allow category leaders to "vote" on supplier classification.

5. Treat the interaction models as dynamic: Rank suppliers, make tough decisions, and give aspirational messages. Do not allow suppliers or yourself to become complacent with the status quo.

Bring SRM to Life

In this chapter, we talked about how to bring SRM to life. To do this, you need to treat the interaction models as dynamic by recognizing that changes occur over time. Use the framework to drive desirable change by giving suppliers consistent and aspirational messages. Be prepared to make the difficult decisions that are needed when less desirable changes happen. Make sure that the governance structure is aligned to the interaction models, that relationship owners are in place, and that communication to suppliers is consistent. By these means, you will help suppliers to help you in the most effective way.

We then went on to discuss the very clear distinction between SRM and category management. The former is about leveraging a company's size and driving desired supplier behavior. The latter is about developing and executing the right strategies for sourcing goods and services—for which the standard tool is the Purchasing Chessboard.

Finally, we discussed how to get started, create momentum, and, importantly, make SRM sustainable. We illustrated this by catching up with our friends at Heartland as they looked back and discussed what they have done to put SRM to work.

The key element that we have not discussed so far is the role of IT in SRM. In the next chapter, we turn our attention to this topic.

The Role of IT in TrueSRM

In our experience, companies often overfocus on elaborate IT tools that are not needed and consume considerable investment resources and management time to implement. It is crucial to consider the basic objectives of an IT implementation before going down that path. The IT tools are there to support the business needs and supplier relationship management. They are not an end in themselves and should not be seen as a substitute for face-to-face and other personal dialogue both with the supplier and internally.

In our experience, there are three key requirements that IT tools need to enable for TrueSRM:

- Tracking supplier performance/compliance
- Enabling internal collaboration
- Enabling external collaboration

These tools need to be deployed in a usable format, with the key elements integrated so that data does not need to be entered multiple times and to enable users to have a common view of the true situation. The organization also needs the discipline to use the tools properly. This is the adoption challenge. It tends to be the most significant issue to overcome.

We will now address each of these elements in turn.

Tracking Supplier Performance/Compliance

Many organizations have basic supplier score cards in place that are used to report performance against key metrics such as contract/Service Level Agreement (SLA) compliance, delivery performance, value-added performance beyond the contract, and so forth. Much of this data is necessarily collected manually, and some via feeds from operational systems where available. These score cards are often created at the category-/business-function level, and then ongoing "production" is delegated to a back-office function that fills in the paperwork. Off-the-shelf spreadsheet or database packages are often used as the enabling tool. To a point, this is an effective reporting solution.

These score card solutions are often combined, or augmented with additional solutions that enable organizations to record and ensure supplier agreement to key policies. The precise need for these varies by industry and geography, but they are increasingly necessary to manage risk.

Recording suppliers' performance and compliance is really a "given." Most organizations have an approach in place. A more valuable SRM solution goes beyond point reporting and provides a more integrated capability across the organization. This feeds relevant performance/compliance information such as supplier segment, supplier overall performance, relevant Key Performance Indicators (KPIs), and corresponding trend information into other business applications, where users deal with suppliers. For example, supplier performance data is highly valuable for users of e-procurement systems. Here, a user should see not only the source, price, availability, and lead time for a catalog item but also performance-related information for the supplier. In particular, the user should be able to see whether there are alternatives. In e-Sourcing, a category manager/buyer needs to have ready access to performance and compliance information, too, as part of the initial prescreening and also for award analysis. If a category-management solution is in place, performance details and trends concerning segmentation and performance of all suppliers in a category should also be visible.

Internal Collaboration

On the customer side, the idea has been around for a long time that a lot of value can be generated if the sales agent talking to a particular customer has a comprehensive "customer history" at hand. When a customer dials into the call center of his insurance company, the agent typically sees information about all of his contracts, his value, his accuracy in on-time payment, his risk score, his recent support calls, e-mails, and letters. Such information helps the agent adjust the communication according to the customer's status. This has spawned the many forms of customer relationship management software.

The functionality to do the same thing in the same way is available on the supplier side, but most organizations have been much slower to put it in place. Given the benefits of ensuring a joined-up approach from dealing with suppliers, the value of doing so is immense. Why not introduce something like this on the supplier side more systematically?

In fact, the information that is immediately available for managing suppliers is often limited to spending, order fulfillment, and score card data. There are often significant challenges in going beyond this. For example:

- Procurement often lacks permission to see sales data if the supplier is also an important customer.

- It sometimes takes weeks of research and dozens of phone calls to stakeholders across multiple sites and business units to get a glimpse of who is talking with a particular supplier about what.

- People are reluctant to log "buy-side" interactions in the same way that is usually a given on the "sell" side.

In our view, the internal-collaboration portion of an SRM solution needs to encompass the following elements:

- *Spending*: "What are we spending with this supplier? What for? Who is buying? What important trends or changes are we seeing?"

- *Contracts*: "What contracts do we have in place with this supplier? When do they expire?"

- *Contract compliance*: "How many issues have been reported where the supplier did not comply with the agreed-upon contract? How severe were these incidents?"

- *Sourcing activities*: "In what sourcing initiatives was the supplier involved? With what success? In case of losing in an initiative, what were the reasons?"

- *Risk, safety, and sustainability compliance*: "Has the supplier confirmed compliance with all policies? Have there been any breaches? Does the organization meet all regulatory requirements?

- *Supplier contact register:* "Who do we know on the supplier side? What do we know about these people? What are their perspectives/agendas?"

- *Internal contact register:* "Who knows this supplier? What kind of relationship is this person having with the supplier? When should one involve her?"

- *Meeting calendar with meeting minutes repository:* "Who has met/is meeting whom from the supplier? What have they been talking about? What has been the outcome?"

- *Documents:* "What are the latest documents we received from this supplier (e.g., company presentations, catalogs, specifications, rate cards)?

- *Wiki:* "What other bits and pieces of information about the supplier has someone from our company picked up that he would like to share with others in the most pragmatic and easy way?"

- *Projects and tasks:* "What projects and tasks are currently underway with this supplier? Who from our side and who from the supplier's side is involved? What is the status? Where are the issues others should know about? What corresponding documents are of potential relevance for others?"

The software functionality to process all this information exists and is available in most organizations. The will, drive, and discipline to make it happen exist less frequently.

Note   There is no reason you can't have the kind of information about suppliers that you no doubt compile about customers. Having a system to collect useful data can be immensely valuable, yet not many organizations have one. This is therefore an easy way to gain a competitive advantage.

Supplier Collaboration

Many organizations today have some form of supplier portal. This opens some functionality of internal collaboration to suppliers. Often, the portal is simply set up to allow suppliers to maintain registration, contact, and payment data. Allowing them to contribute actively and update additional information, as well as jointly execute projects and tasks, is a key extra step. In our view, the supplier portal portion of an SRM solution needs to encompass the following elements as a minimum:

- *Performance visibility*: In areas where a company wants to establish a truly collaborative relationship, it could share all ratings and conclusions with suppliers. Buyers often hesitate to share positive performance feedback in order not to strengthen the negotiation position of a supplier. We believe that the benefits of positive feedback usually far outweigh the risks.

- *Issue visibility, commenting, and resolution*: Even if a buyer does not want to share all performance information with a certain supplier, everyone benefits from giving a supplier immediate feedback on specific issues through e-mail notifications and alerts in the supplier portal. Even better solutions allow a supplier to comment on such issues. Sometimes, an issue (like late delivery) might have been caused by forces outside of the supplier's control and should therefore not overly damage its performance rating. If the collaboration solution supports task management, corresponding tasks for issue resolution can be set up with responsibilities and deadlines for improved resolution monitoring. This, then, supports the traditional approaches of direct contact and conversation to resolve issues. It should not be a substitute for these things.

- *Reverse feedback*: In the interest of collaborative improvement in a relationship, it is a good idea to allow your suppliers to provide feedback about your performance. Technically, this requires the setup of corresponding surveys, permissions, and linking to the supplier portal. Giving the supplier the ability to provide this information via a portal is a useful supplement to the typical one-off, anonymous 360-degree surveys that organizations often put in place. Of course, the propensity of suppliers to give open and honest feedback without anonymity is an interesting test of relationship strength.

It is also possible to extend the scope of the portal beyond these minimum elements to include facilities for joint innovation. These would allow the supplier to submit innovative ideas that could be discussed/approved. You'd then follow a stage-gate process for tracking implementation. Such an approach can be a useful addition. However, we cannot stress enough that IT tools do not produce innovation. True innovation typically requires effective dialogue with the supplier, a commitment to cocreation, and the ability to make decisions. In the absence of such a process, way-too-many potential innovations just get ignored.

Clearly, all external collaboration via systems has technical challenges. As soon as a company opens certain doors in the firewall, substantial IT security implications require expert attention. Permission management in internal collaboration is in many companies already challenging enough, as the more strategic a relationship with a supplier gets, the more sensitive it becomes. The biggest challenge comes from an inability of most systems to deal with a multidimensional permission matrix. Most systems are still very transaction oriented. A user either has permission to access a transaction or not. The more comprehensively we do SRM, the more it becomes necessary to define and administer permissions holistically. With external participants, the permission management becomes even more challenging. One way to sidestep these issues is to manage collaboration in a separately hosted "clean room" environment that is outside the firewalls of both the customer and the supplier. Data is kept safe within the clean room and the issues of allowing third parties direct system access are avoided.

Tip   Use a virtual "clean room" to manage collaboration with suppliers. You can supply the relevant data there without offering full access to your IT systems.

Usability and Adoption

If you build a system with all the components just outlined, you will have built a great repository of information, easily accessible to everyone (with corresponding permissions, of course). An ideal SRM solution not only collects information from various other systems but also provides outbound interfaces, making essential SRM-related information available to other systems. In times where most business applications have become browser enabled, it just takes a little imagination to envision a workplace where a user, whenever she sees supplier-related information on her screen, can hover over the supplier name and see a display of the essentials about this supplier (e.g., segment, alerts, and so forth) along with a link to a more detailed dashboard if needed.

The Adoption Challenge

Now, we need to get users to actually use the SRM solution. Far too many IT solutions suffer from poor adoption. This is often for a simple reason: the users do not see the benefits. In our view, a useful SRM solution should encompass the following usability elements to support adoption:

- *Maximum user configurability*: All our attempts to collect and display as much information about a supplier as possible can easily lead to a situation where we show way-too-much information to a user, which might overwhelm and cause confusion. An ideal solution comes in a very lightweight form in the beginning but then allows the user to select the elements of interest that he wants to pop up next time automatically. Similar to the earlier-mentioned difficulties with multidimensional permission management that most systems today still have, the same applies with the requirements for ideal information configurability. It is more than likely that a category manager would like to see much more detail about one or two key suppliers instantly, a little less for some others and just some lightweight information about the rest. This triage approach is essential to get user buy in.

- *Proactive alerting*: How many reports do you have access to? And how many do you actually look at daily, weekly, or at least monthly? It is too common an occurrence that having great information in a system does not necessarily mean it finds its way to the user who should be aware of it. An ideal SRM solution allows the admin as well as the user to define flexibly configurable alerts that shoot an e-mail to selected user(s) under certain conditions (e.g., "Supplier XYZ's performance trend is negative"). The configurability again needs to be multidimensional.

- *Visual analytics*: Not only do long lists of data easily create an information overload, they also often make it difficult to see the forest for the trees. Advanced visual analytics is not about creating nice-looking graphics but all about transforming data in a way that makes it easier to recognize the meaning or identify areas that should get closer attention.

- *Personal information integration*: Let's face it: if you are a supplier manager, you probably have tons of information on your hard disk/network drive and in your e-mail. Getting additional information from others? Great! Sharing your own information? Extra effort! Even with sophisticated incentives and penalties, it is hard to overcome this natural reluctance to spend time on something that only benefits you personally in a limited way. Sure, the organization benefits, but the individual person is not getting rewarded. This is why we believe a lot of success is dependent on how easy we make it for people to share information. Studies show that average office workers spend 80 percent of their daily IT time working with their own personal information (e-mail, address book, calendar, chat). If you want the user to share, for example, an attachment just received from a strategic supplier, you should not expect her to download it, then open a browser, then find the right site for this supplier, and then upload the file and provide contextual information. Instead, you'd enable smart integration with the user's personal information by allowing her to "drag and drop" this attachment right into the repository.

- *Active adoption management*: Many systems, if they are not essential for daily operations, die a slow but certain death. We just explained a couple of reasons for this, but there is one more, which has nothing to do with the system itself but with the way it gets rolled out into the organization, how its usage is monitored, whether and how frequently news and success stories get communicated, and to what extent users get the right level of support they need.

Note You have to work to get a new IT solution adopted. It won't happen on its own. Worse, if it's the kind of thing people rarely go into, it will die an early death.

We have now discussed the key IT requirements for TrueSRM to enable performance and compliance tracking as well as to support both internal and external collaboration. The challenges are not technical ones. They are more to do with having the will to put the systems in place and then to use them rigorously. Much of the necessary functionality and disciplines mirror what your company already probably does on the "sell" side with its customers through active customer relationship management (CRM) systems. It is often beneficial to make the case for following the necessary disciplines in these terms by stressing the symmetry between the disciplines needed for good CRM and good supplier management.

It is now time to return to the story at Heartland. You will recall that the group has just been interviewed by a well-known journalist who is trying to identify the reasons for their great success. The attentive reader will have noticed that IT systems were not on the list of key success factors that the journalist captured. Let's now catch up with Laura and Thomas to see what role, if any, IT has played in the story.

Heartland Contemplates IT's Contribution to SRM

A short time after the magazine interview, Thomas was in his office late one afternoon. Laura walked in to debrief him quickly on a meeting that had taken place that day with Product Maniacs, the company's new supplier. It had suggested a way to put one of the core Heartland brands up in lights legally and simultaneously on the Empire State Building, the Shard in London, the Eiffel Tower, and the Burj Khalifa in Dubai.

However, Thomas was preoccupied. He asked, "Laura, are you aware of this discussion to overhaul our entire Enterprise Resource Planning (ERP) infrastructure? There is a suggestion that we need to spend tens of millions of dollars that I am sure will become hundreds of millions. There seems to be no real business case for doing this, though, other than a claim that we will get better management information on external spending and make our back-office processes more efficient. Oh, and there is also a claim that it will better enable our activities with suppliers." He flipped to the back page of the document that was on his desk and then said, "They are claiming a business case. It will all be justified by suppliers giving us savings as a result of all this IT!"

"I had heard some discussion," said Laura, "but I have not seen that document. I'm surprised I never got it or had a chance to comment."

"It's labelled preliminary," Thomas told her, as he handed it over. "It came from IT. I probably shouldn't have it yet," he commented with a smile. "Let's just say that someone handed it to me. I like to know what is being discussed before it goes anywhere. Do you agree with this approach? Will it help us to continue to deliver SRM?"

"We don't need it," Laura answered. "There might be other reasons to overhaul the ERP, although I am not sure I know what they are, but I am not pushing for it. Most of the things we need to do, we are fine with."

"Yes, we have never really discussed IT as a big part of SRM," suggested Thomas.

"Well," said Laura, "if I think purely about our IT needs for supplier management rather than for category management, compliance, and transactions processing, then what we really require are tools that enable three things: performance measurement, internal collaboration, and external collaboration. We then just need to be able to use them and make sure that people are disciplined to do so."

Thomas turned his chair more fully toward her but said nothing.

Laura continued. "For performance measurement, we have put in place simple score cards for each significant supplier. The score cards are maintained by the relevant supplier lead within Procurement. They are then filed on a simple wiki site. It's basic IT technology, but they are fit for our purpose. We have some feeds to capture online data such as missed deliveries for direct suppliers, but most of the information is maintained by people in the business. It's not captured in the systems anyway so there is little alternative available. In any event, we use the process of populating the scorecards to trigger conversations about performance, which are used as input for our rankings. It's not fully automated, nor could it ever be. It works and is fit for purpose. We also encourage an approach based on the 80–20 rule, which simplifies things too."

"The 80–20 rule always worries some of our colleagues," said Thomas. "They think it means we are ignoring critical incidents."

"You know we don't do that, Thomas. What I mean is that we do not try to split hairs over relative supplier performance. It's a bit like employee performance in so many ways. I am not interested if a supplier's performance is 53rd percentile vs. 54th percentile. I am interested if a supplier is consistently in the top 20 percent, the middle 60 percent, or the bottom 20 percent. Our approach to measurement enables us to make that level of differentiation. Investing in doing more is not going to be helpful and will just be a waste of money."

"So, our current approach is good enough, then?" Thomas inquired.

"Yes. We then make sure that the score card information is available to key people internally, of course. You already have access to it on your executive dashboard."

"I sure do. I even look at it before meetings," he grinned.

"To enable that internal collaboration and data access, we have just deployed the CRM tool that our sales force uses to keep tabs on customer contacts, relationships, and meetings. The key issue is not the system functionality. The ability to log contacts with suppliers and so forth is fairly straightforward. Sharing the data is also easy. The challenge is getting people (especially executives) to populate the information."

"I know," said Thomas. He laughed. "By the way, who is making sure the notes from that Product Maniacs meeting today get on there?"

"I have found that the best way to get people to do it is to ask what's the best thing to do after a customer meeting. Of course, they all agree that updating CRM and circulating notes is crucial. They all agree, too, that meeting a customer without being briefed is not smart. So, why is it any different if we are meeting a key supplier?"

"People get that logic. I know," agreed Thomas.

"Exactly," said Laura. "We then have the supplier portal, of course. That provides the basic functionality for suppliers to update core data with us and confirm policy compliance. It also provides a means to have structured dialogue on issues. I am going to extend it to include conversations on supplier-driven innovations. I am a little wary, though, of it just becoming an easy mechanical tool. You know what can happen. The supplier can dream up numerous things, and then just stick them on the portal. Suppliers may feel that they have to give us large numbers of ideas with no obvious reference to their quality and practicality. We for our part may just get swamped with all these ideas. That would not be very helpful. We are still working through how to make sure that any additions here support the way we drive supplier innovation rather than becoming a pure self-serving 'numbers' process."

"The key thing is the innovations we actually implement and the benefit we get," suggested Thomas, "not what gets logged on the system."

"Absolutely," agreed Laura. "We are seeing major innovations already, of course, which surface through collaboration with the right suppliers."

"So, there is very little we need to do with the SRM systems?" asked Thomas.

"I think so," said Laura. "A bit of evolutionary enhancement will be good. But you don't need to overhaul the whole ERP system. I certainly will not be prepared to sign up for more supplier savings from doing that in any case!"

You Can Build It

As the Heartland story showed, a useful SRM solution:

1. Is based on a state-of-the-art IT architecture for scalability and ease of administration

2. Collects and provides all relevant data and comes with appropriate measures to correct, complete, and enrich otherwise-insufficient data

3. Provides information to all users in the easiest possible way (ideally without the need for users to access multiple keys on the keyboard and without multiple system clicks)

4. Leverages advanced statistics to allow users to derive business intelligence beyond the obvious

5. Automates low-value-add tasks for improved adoption

6. Stipulates collaboration (document sharing, wiki, chat, and so on) and best-practice sharing in the form of templates across the organization and for use with suppliers

7. Avoids information overload, leveraging advanced visual analytics, and push reporting

Does such an SRM solution already exist? Not that we are aware of. At least, not in a way that is integrated across different applications with shared data and end-to-end functionality. SRM system implementations have often not advanced much beyond stand-alone point implementations of a contract database, performance score card, or portal for suppliers to register their details. There is a major opportunity for organizations to move beyond this basic state of play.

Is it possible to build it? Yes. Nothing described in this chapter is rocket science. The IT functionality is often available, and in fact many organizations are already deploying much of it for managing customer relationships! The challenge has less to do with the basic functionality and more to do with the wherewithal to integrate the different point solutions that are often already in place, and then to drive usability and adoption.

Large IT Investments Are Unnecessary

In this chapter, we discussed how IT can support TrueSRM most effectively major investment in systems is usually not necessary. Using existing functionalities in a disciplined way, while keeping sight of the overall objective, is the most effective approach.

In the next chapter, we turn back to that overall objective. We will look at what is "different" for a business that has implemented TrueSRM. For, the whole point of doing this is to be more successful as a business. We will take a look at how this is so. We will also catch up for a final time with the story at Heartland—and see how different its business becomes as a result of fully implementing TrueSRM.

The "Difference" You Get from TrueSRM

Companies introducing, applying, and living TrueSRM will undergo fundamental changes. These changes will be necessary to stay competitive in the market. Similar to the introduction of category management over the past two decades, TrueSRM will separate the leaders from the laggards. Done right, it will help companies to leverage suppliers and harness the energy that is out there in the supplier market. The changes associated with the introduction will be felt:

- Within procurement
- Across functions
- Across hierarchy levels
- By suppliers
- By competitors

Let's look at each in turn.

Changes Felt Within Procurement

Procurement teams will have to understand the clear separation between category management and supplier relationship management once the changes are implemented. Perhaps this can best be achieved by first making it crystal clear what exactly category management is. We have elaborated on this in Chapter 8 and recommend *The Purchasing Chessboard* as a read for those who would like to dive deeper into this topic. Once category management is clearly defined, the more challenging task of clarifying supplier relationship management can be approached. We are confident that this book encompasses the core elements and success factors of SRM, but, in most cases, companies will not have many of their own success stories to build upon when entering this territory.

Once the separation between category management and SRM is understood, new roles and responsibilities have to be accepted. That will be uncomfortable to many. While in the current state, most category managers might assume that they are also managing the supplier relationship, TrueSRM will bundle the relationship management. For many procurement team members, this will mean having to navigate in some kind of matrix with both category and relationship aspects being managed. Life will become more complicated than it is today.

The most probable, drastic change in Procurement will be the need to identify different priorities and employ different skill sets. By focusing attention on suppliers in the Critical Cluster, many tasks that appear to be "supplier management" today will be eliminated. Team members who currently perform these tasks will not necessarily be the ones with the right skills to work with suppliers in the Influence, Integrate, and Invest interaction models.

Changes Felt Across Functions

SRM is a cross-functional top-management task. One might have said the same thing about strategic sourcing and category management five years ago. The key difference is that while strategic sourcing and category management are cross-functional and procurement led, SRM is cross-functional as well but might be led by functions outside of procurement.

Let's take a more detailed look at which function is leading SRM. For the Harvest, Improve, Sustain, Mitigate, and Develop supplier interaction models, the distribution of roles will not be too different from strategic sourcing and category management. Procurement's role will be to facilitate quarterly reviews with suppliers and to coach suppliers in providing meaningful and consistent progress reports. Other functions will support this process, but Procurement will lead the way.

For the Bail Out interaction model, it is hard to make a generalization on the distribution of roles. Depending on the nature of the problem with the Bail Out supplier, a specific task force will be put in place. The leader of the task force will ideally be recruited from the function or discipline that has the critical competence to fix the problem. So, if the supplier has a manufacturing issue, the leader of the effort would come from internal manufacturing, or if the supplier has a financial issue, corporate finance would take the lead.

Remember that a key mission of TrueSRM is to focus attention on those few suppliers that really matter in the long run. Relationships to suppliers that fall into this category would be managed with the Influence, Invest, and Integrate interaction models. For these interaction models, specific governance models would be put in place and Procurement would typically be more a contributor than a leader in this context.

Changes Felt Across Hierarchy Levels

Earlier we stated that SRM is a cross-functional top management task. In line with the cross-functional discussion, top management is unlikely to get involved in decisions regarding suppliers in the Harvest, Improve, Sustain, Mitigate, and Develop supplier interaction models. If suppliers in these interaction models happen to be significant suppliers in terms of the amount of business transacted, then top management might occasionally join quarterly review meetings to emphasize messages that are prepared by the Procurement-led cross-functional teams. However, the intensity of the interaction will be significantly lower than for suppliers in the Critical Cluster, irrespective of the amount of business transacted.

Suppliers in the Bail Out interaction model will typically be highly relevant for top management, and, very often, top management might have put the supplier into that interaction model. Since the Bail Out task forces need to operate at high speed and far beyond the usual boundaries of doing business, top management will be key for opening doors.

The most regular top management involvement is likely to be seen in the Influence, Invest, and Integrate interaction models. In many companies, the key challenge will be to connect ongoing top management activities to the SRM efforts. A serious TrueSRM program will limit the freedom of top management to reach out to their counterparts at suppliers at will.

Note If you are serious about implementing TrueSRM, senior executives will no longer have the freedom to contact suppliers whenever they want without serious internal alignment being achieved first.

Changes Felt By Suppliers

Suppliers should generally appreciate their customers embracing TrueSRM, as it brings clarity into the overall relationship. For suppliers in the Harvest, Improve, Sustain, Mitigate, and Develop interaction models, the relationship will be transactional. There will be clear expectations regarding what needs to be done by the next quarterly milestone review, and good performance will be rewarded. At the same time, the supplier will not need to dedicate resources to bringing the relationship to a place it will never go—because there is mutual clarity on what the relationship really is.

Suppliers in the Bail Out interaction model will receive the attention they deserve. What might have resulted in finger pointing in the past is replaced by a swift corrective intervention by the customer's task force. A smart supplier will fully cooperate with the task force, as ultimately it can only win and learn from it.

Suppliers in Influence, Invest, and Integrate will first need to understand the unique position they have been assigned. They will have the opportunity to grow, make game-changing moves, and build winning ecosystems. In the end, the customer is competing for mind share, and, since this is a limited resource, it will always be an investment and account management decision by the supplier whether or not to fully engage. What should be clear to everybody involved is that the Integrate supplier interaction model, especially, can only work if both parties are fully engaged. A supplier that is not ready should communicate this proactively to avoid wasting its customer's time and resources.

Changes Felt by Competitors

Competitors of a company like Heartland Consolidated Industries that fully embrace TrueSRM will struggle to understand what hit them. They will wonder what Heartland did to become so much more competitive:

- Did they hire a new breed of managers?

- Did they put some new type of innovation process in place?

- Is it a different kind of incentive system for internal people?

- Are they getting some form of external help, maybe from a consulting firm?

- Is it the new CEO who brought some magic tricks from his former employer?

- Is there something we did wrong to fall out of favor with our key suppliers?

As readers of this book, you know the answer. By introducing TrueSRM, Heartland has taken the game to an entirely new level. Managing the relationship with thousands of suppliers has always been a losing proposition. What Heartland did right was putting suppliers into the right buckets and defining clearly differentiated approaches for each bucket. This allowed Heartland to deprioritize suppliers that are useful but don't make a difference in the grand scheme of things. With this, Heartland freed up management capacity to focus on those few suppliers that really matter to them. Once those select-few suppliers recognized this, Heartland got a lot more out of them than any of Heartland's competitors. This, in turn, sparked a virtuous cycle that made Heartland the number-one place for any ambitious supplier to go to because working with the company got it the best chance at growing fast and profitably.

With this, let us conclude by looking at an article written by Elisabeth Huttich two years after her first interview with Thomas Sutter and Laura Braida. It was published in the *Global Economy* as a "briefing" piece.

Heartland's Secret Sauce

How a Dull Consumer Goods Company Reinvented Itself to Become the Darling of the Stock Market... and Others.

By Elisabeth Huttich

The Star of Fort Wayne

Taxi drivers are often a reliable indicator for the mood in a community. So when your correspondent arrived at Fort Wayne's cozy little airport, she did not head for the rental-car booths but got into one of the very few cabs available. After looking quickly at me through the rearview mirror, the driver asked, "Are you coming here to work for Heartland?" Over the next 20 minutes, he talked about how much Fort Wayne had changed over the past years thanks to the company.

First, there were all these smart kids moving to Fort Wayne to work for Heartland. He called them the Silicon Valley crowd. Obviously, Heartland must pay them very well, for what other reason would they move from California to Indiana? Second, lots of companies were opening up offices in Fort Wayne and they surely must have something to do with Heartland. He had overheard their executives discussing contracts with Heartland in his cab on their way to and from the airport. Then there was a lot of construction work going on, most notably on Heartland's new campus. That was very good for some of his buddies who were in the industry. And finally, there were the prices of houses. His own house, which he had inherited from his grandparents, had more than tripled in value over the past five years. He could sell it for a handsome amount, but then all the other houses seem to have gotten more expensive too, so he wondered whether that would be a good idea.

How did Heartland transform not only Fort Wayne, Indiana, but also itself? How is it that Fort Wayne is mentioned in business dailies more often than Cupertino, Mountain View, or Menlo Park? How did a formerly dull food-products company that was better known for causing obesity than excitement become the most desired employer for business school graduates?

Many attempts have been made at answering these questions and the latest count yields eight books on the topic. Emma Jenkins, Heartland's notoriously tight-lipped spokesperson, has dismissed all of those books as inaccurate. As a correspondent, I have been on the Heartland story for more than two years after conducting an interview with Thomas Sutter, Heartland's CEO, and Laura Braida, then the company's CPO, or chief procurement officer, and now its COO, or chief operations officer, after the recent departure of Rick Fiore. To date, this interview is still regarded by many as giving the most relevant clues on what makes Heartland tick.

Heartland's executives are not eager to share their secret sauce with the rest of the world. Both Sutter and Braida regularly give interviews, but they are very skillful at avoiding giving insights into how they are running the company. Heartland's wider executive team does not talk to media, not even off the record. This left me to conduct my research for this article largely based on interviews with former executives and suppliers.

Even Suppliers Rave About Heartland

Usually, suppliers are very reluctant to talk about their customers publicly. When they talk off the record, the tone is usually critical. Heartland is different. One of the suppliers known to work very closely with the company is Caledonian Packaging, the global-packaging giant headquartered in Edinburgh. Calum Drummond, Caledonian's CEO, is a towering and imposing man who has hardly given any interviews in his 15 years of leading the company, yet he was willing to talk about the relationship with Heartland in general and Thomas Sutter specifically.

Caledonian Packaging is a family-owned business that was founded by Drummond's great-grand-uncle in the early 20th century. The executive explained that in his view, unlike many publicly listed companies, Caledonian has always taken an extremely long-term perspective about every business relationship it entertains. For an average food product, the packaging makes up less than 5 percent of the overall product cost. And it is very difficult to replace the packaging because of the regulatory approvals required, such as with the FDA in America.

So, Caledonian's approach typically is, in his words, "Simply to do a good job, provide flawless quality, and help our customers to achieve what they want. Over the past 20 years, this has mostly been about dealing with smaller lot sizes. Think yogurt. When I was a child, there were maybe 20 different brand and flavor combinations of yogurt in a grocery store. Today, it can easily be over a hundred in an average supermarket. We have had to become very efficient at making short production runs of yogurt lids in all kinds of colors and layouts."

Drummond further explained that many of his big customers have hired armies of consultants and MBAs in procurement principally to negotiate much more advantageous commercial terms and squeeze his profit margins.

I asked him for his views on this. He felt it is OK and that it keeps Caledonian at the top of its game commercially. "But then you have to ask yourself, What does a consumer goods company get out of its packaging supplier? Is it just about nickeling and diming us, or is there more? A smart man might reckon that the packaging is what talks to the consumer at the point of sale. And this is what my friend Thomas Sutter instinctively understood. He could have done what all his competitors are doing and set his blood hounds on us. Laura Braida, who was leading their procurement, is pretty sharp. She, for sure, could have squeezed 2 percent savings out of us, no doubt about that. But they went for the smart packaging innovation with us. And everybody now understands how to work with their packaging supplier."

Drummond's comments about Heartland were borne out by other off-the-record conversations with suppliers in the industry. They were reluctant to talk openly for fear of offending other customers who behave differently from Heartland.

Heartland Is a Business Transformed

With Sutter at its helm, Heartland has become nothing less than America's career hotbed. Not only is the company the employer of choice for business school graduates, it has also become the prime target of headhunters. Companies from just about every industry want to replicate the Heartland success story by bringing the company's people on board. The most famous Heartland alumnus is, of course, Rick Fiore, formerly Heartland's COO, now CEO of Detroit Motors, America's second-biggest maker of passenger cars and light trucks. Fiore's family still lives in Fort Wayne, and he and Sutter are frequently seen together doing long runs on early Saturday and Sunday mornings.

Asked what they chat about during these runs, Fiore claims that Sutter is paying him back. "When Thomas joined Heartland from Autowerke, he knew nothing about consumer goods and I was his tutor. I believe Thomas is still grateful for that. So, when I was approached by Detroit Motors, Thomas spent a lot of time explaining the key success factors of a carmaker to me. He still knows a lot about the industry and I go to him to test ideas that I am pondering."

Fiore is clearly proud of his close connection to Sutter. "What Thomas brought to Heartland was focus. Focus on what really matters." Fiore explained that Sutter is very good at identifying winners and ignoring everything else. He says that, in essence, Heartland, under Sutter's leadership, is all about a differentiated customer experience. This means that each of Heartland's products or services needs to leave a lasting positive experience in the customer's mind. And, in Fiore's words: "That experience needs to be way beyond anything that Heartland's competitors can offer."

Suppliers Have Been the Crucial Ingredient

Most businesses claim to be able to offer a differentiated customer experience. What is interesting about Heartland is how it says it has done that. The point that Fiore stresses is that effective supplier management, or what he describes as "TrueSRM," or more fully "True Supplier Relationship Management," has been critical for achieving that differentiated customer experience.

This perspective is not just hype. The company's success has come from a combination of the chief executive's vision and effective supplier relationships. Fiore cites the second-generation frozen-food packaging as an example where innovation involved leveraging multiple networked supplier relationships. This now includes the use of semiconductors and LCDs as an integral part of the packaging to improve the safety of food handling by monitoring temperature. Heartland had already introduced packaging that changes color once it has been out of the freezer too long. This had been developed in cooperation with Caledonian. You might have thought that this would do the job. Not so for Heartland under Sutter. Fiore explained that Sutter "has this laser focus and thinks many steps ahead. He always warned us that competitors would soon come up with something comparable." So, the CEO drove the creation of a tripartite relationship between Heartland, Caledonian, and a small Silicon Valley start-up to work time and again on more advanced solutions. This led to the development of yet another level of ice cream packaging that has a printed display telling you how many more minutes you can keep the ice cream outside of the freezer. This has been a great success for Heartland. Up to then, no one had thought that you could make semiconductors and LCD displays into a part of packaging by printing them cheaply. As we have reported before, Heartland's competitors are suffering intensely. Their ice cream and frozen food are considered by many to be unsafe in light of this new packaging.

Will the Changes Last?

The question is whether these changes at Heartland are more than skin-deep. Will they outlast Sutter? Fiore thinks they will. He explained: "Of course Thomas cannot be everywhere at once, which is why he is building operating models that force people to focus." He talked about the interface with suppliers. A company as big as Heartland will always have tens of thousands of suppliers or, if you take a single business unit, it will be a couple of thousand. But among this huge number of suppliers, only a handful of them really matter. In Fiore's view, what Sutter and Braida did was to select a few suppliers to really focus on for relationship building and deprioritized all the others. The hard part of this exercise was the deprioritizing. According to Fiore, people were very skeptical initially, but with the first successes coming in, the mood changed very quickly. "Now, everybody at Heartland gets it."

Consumers around the globe seem to agree with Fiore. The entire consumer-goods and retail industry is undergoing changes that are unprecedented since the introduction of the refrigerator and the supermarket. It is useful to think of the innovations Heartland is introducing as some kind of chain reaction. Its first-generation smart ice cream packaging increased consumers' awareness of the importance of uninterrupted freezing by showing them when this had been compromised. The second-generation packaging would go on to become so effective that consumers could tell if they had left the product out of the freezer for too long, and it gave a warning before that point was reached that the temperature was in danger of becoming compromised.

Developing World Teaches the Developed World

Then came the third wave of supplier-based innovation, based on the *dabbawalas* working in India. Now a familiar sight in megacities, this new group of delivery people use carts or bicycles to transport goods. Heartland introduced this role to deliver products directly from the supplier to the consumer. In a recent report, A. T. Kearney, a global management consulting firm, argued that the dabbawalas working for Heartland have been highlighted as a key competitive advantage for Heartland and a real game changer in the supply chain for food. Trips to supermarkets have become the exception for city dwellers, as Heartland's dabbawalas get you everything you need on short notice. On top of its environmental impact, the introduction of dabbawalas has been the tipping point for Heartland, with their market shares and revenues skyrocketing while those of their competitors have gone into a collective nosedive.

Rumor has it that Sutter and Braida came up with the idea to introduce dabbawalas for distribution to consumers during consecutive business meetings in Mumbai and New York City. In Mumbai, they saw the original dabbawalas delivering lunch boxes to office workers from their family homes to their offices. In Manhattan, they saw bicycle messengers and compared them to the dabbawala rickshaws that are a familiar sight in Mumbai. They then half-jokingly speculated what dabbawalas could do in New York. Days after having this idea, they were discussing implementation plans in earnest with potential suppliers.

Sutter and Braida took a big gamble. By going direct to consumers and bypassing retailers, they were jeopardizing the very foundation of Heartland's business. But then, a glance at what had happened to the music and book businesses made the case very clear to Heartland's executive board. Sutter is rumored to have said, "If we don't do it, somebody else is going to do it. And I would rather be in control of our destiny than be at the mercy of some external forces." In hindsight, one can conclude that Sutter was right. Heartland's direct distribution business through the dabbawala supplier relationships grew much faster than its revenues with retailers. And with retailers closing down outlets everywhere, they are becoming increasingly obsolete to Heartland.

Living the Dream

Konstantin Bauer, my personal dabbawala in my hometown of Munich, explained how he feels about his Heartland-enabled side job. He studied physics at the Technical University and has always worked to finance his studies. Bauer describes his office jobs: "On top of being boring, they left me out of shape. You know, I sit in the lab, I sit at my desk in the dorm studying, and I sat in an office. Days got too short to do exercise. When I was still in high school, I would work out two or three hours a day; here in Munich I sometimes did not do any exercise for two or three days in a row."

Now, Bauer works as an independent dabbawala supplier for three to four hours a day. He has an app on his smartphone that tells him when and where to pick up the deliveries for his tour. His area is a bit suburban, so he uses a hand cart. Bauer told me, "At the start of the tour, the cart I push is so heavy that I can hardly lift the handles. But since I am usually running while I deliver the items, it is a great workout that makes my muscles ache and it feels fantastic. Most of my friends are dabbawalas as well. Each of us has a different style. Some of them have even started to balance those large trays on their heads that the original dabbawalas in India are using."

Bauer always works in the same neighborhood, which means that most people know him and he knows them. Some even put their keys in a secret place for him so that he can put their groceries into the fridge for them. Of course, as he recounts, those are the ones that give the biggest tips. This system is very much based on trust.

Bauer explains that "the pay as a Heartland dabbawala is very good, but then there is also this coolness factor. We get these fancy outfits and all of us are really fit and trim. In Munich, there are now even pretend dabbawalas who wear the outfit in the clubs. That is something we don't do."

Asked about his aspirations after graduation, Konstantin Bauer has a very clear idea: "I want to join the research division of Heartland in Fort Wayne. This is the one place to be for a scientist. I spent a day on the premises last summer when I travelled the Midwest. Even their old site was pretty cool, but the new one they are building right now blows your mind. It will be ready just when I graduate."

Building New Ecosystems with Suppliers

Bauer is very conscious that he is doing something special. What he is dreaming about is opening new doors for Heartland. He firmly believes that in the future the food industry and the pharmaceutical industry will converge. "Let's face it, what the pharmaceutical industry has been doing over the past 150 years is pumping the human body full of chemicals and finding out in a trial-and-error process how it will respond to them. And then it sold the resulting approved drugs in a one-size-fits-all model through pharmacies. Yet we know that depending on gender, age, weight, and many other personal factors, everybody reacts to drugs in a different way."

In Bauer's vision, each of us will wear a smart device, for example a watch, that will monitor our bodily functions on an ongoing basis. This device will be linked to an intelligent health care system, a virtual doctor with unlimited knowledge so to speak. If some of your parameters go out of predefined boundaries, a device in your home will custom make drugs for your very personal conditions at this specific point in time. Bauer asked me to imagine this like a very sophisticated 3D printer that prints a power bar for you.

If Bauer and Heartland are right, then the ability to engineer new relationships with suppliers and create innovative ecosystems will be crucial for success in the future. This does not only apply in the food industry but also in a far more broad scope. Companies cannot hope to create all the innovations that they need purely internally. They need to partner, focus on the handful of key relationships that have the right strategic potential, and work relentlessly to build the right ecosystems.

Heartland may well be the one company that can pull this off. They have proven to be willing to overcome established beliefs and they are able to create ecosystems that are changing entire industries. Bauer knows that in order to get into Heartland he will have to compete against the best graduates of the world's most prestigious academic institutions. He is studying night and day to get there. The vision that Heartland has created is why many of the best and the brightest are doing likewise. It is only a matter of time before the rest of the world copies Heartland.

A Final Word

In this book, we have introduced and explained TrueSRM—a way of working with suppliers that is strongly differentiated based on performance and strategic potential. Companies need to focus most of their attention on the handful of relationships that have the high strategic potential to really make a difference in their competitiveness. As we see more and more dysfunctional change across industries, the ability to harness these Critical Cluster relationships will be of more and more importance. As the boundaries between industries increasingly converge, no single company will internally possess all of the capabilities that are needed for future success.

Done well, TrueSRM is the key to staying relevant in a changing world. It goes far beyond the concerns of "traditional" procurement. We implore you to embrace it.

Index

Get the eBook for only $10!

Now you can take the weightless companion with you anywhere, anytime. Your purchase of this book entitles you to 3 electronic versions for only $10.

This Apress title will prove so indispensible that you'll want to carry it with you everywhere, which is why we are offering the eBook in 3 formats for only $10 if you have already purchased the print book.

Convenient and fully searchable, the PDF version enables you to easily find and copy code—or perform examples by quickly toggling between instructions and   applications. The MOBI format is ideal for your Kindle, while the ePUB can be utilized on a variety of mobile devices.

Go to www.apress.com/promo/tendollars to purchase your companion eBook.

Other Apress Business Titles You Will Find Useful

The CPO
Schuh/Strohmer/Easton/
Scharlach/Scharbert
978-1-4302-4962-7

CFO Techniques
Guzik
978-1-4302-3756-3

**When to Hire—or Not
Hire—a Consultant**
Orr/Orr
978-1-4302-4734-0

**Eliminating Waste in
Business**
Orr/Orr
978-1-4302-6088-2

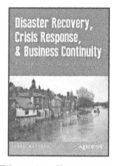

**Disaster Recovery,
Crisis Response, and
Business Continuity**
Watters
978-1-4302-6406-4

**Reputation, Stock
Price, and You**
Kossovsky
978-1-4302-4890-3

**Commercializing
Innovation**
Schaufeld
978-1-4302-6352

Improving Profit
Cleland
978-1-4302-6307-4

**Due Diligence and the
Business Transaction**
Berkman
978-1-4302-5086-9

Available at www.apress.com

9 781430 262596